Grand Theory in Folkloristics

ENCOUNTERS: Explorations in Folklore and Ethnomusicology
Michael Dylan Foster and Ray Cashman, Editors

A *Journal of Folklore Research* Book

Grand Theory in Folkloristics

Edited by Lee Haring

INDIANA UNIVERSITY PRESS

Bloomington and Indianapolis

This book is a publication of

Indiana University Press
Office of Scholarly Publishing
Herman B Wells Library 350
1320 East 10th Street
Bloomington, Indiana 47405 USA

iupress.indiana.edu

The paper used in this publication meets the minimum requirements of the American
National Standard for Information Sciences—Permanence of Paper for Printed Library
Materials, ANSI Z39.48–1992.

Manufactured in the United States of America

Library of Congress Cataloging-in-Publication Data

Names: Haring, Lee, editor.
Title: Grand theory in folkloristics / edited by Lee Haring.
Description: Bloomington : Indiana University Press, 2016. | Series:
    Encounters : explorations in folklore and ethnomusicology | Includes
    bibliographical references and index.
Identifiers: LCCN 2016019302| ISBN 9780253024398 (pbk. : alk. paper) |
    ISBN 9780253024428 (ebook)
Subjects: LCSH: Folklore–United States–Philosophy. | Folklore–Study and
    teaching–United States.
Classification: LCC GR105 .G727 2016 | DDC 398.20973–dc23 LC record available at
https://lccn.loc.gov/2016019302

1 2 3 4 5   21 20 19 18 17 16

On the cover: Gustave Baumann, *Grand Canyon*, 1934, color woodcut, 12 11/16 x 12 13/16 in.
Collection of the New Mexico Museum of Art. Museum purchase with funds raised by
the School of American Research, 1952 (903.23G). Copyright © New Mexico Museum
of Art. Photo by Blair Clark.

Contents

AFTERWORDS

Preface: Theorizing Grand Theory in Folkloristics

THIS BOOK IS an expanded edition of a *Journal of Folklore Research* special issue published in 2008. That original issue had a long history and, for a slim volume, has made remarkably expansive ripples in the disciplinary pool of folkloristics. The time is right, we feel, to republish the articles collected therein because the questions they raise are just as critical today as they were almost a decade ago. What is "grand theory"? Do folklorists in fact lack grand theory? Why should it matter (or not) for folklore studies? How does/should theory inform our research? The chapters that follow fervently address these questions and many more, exploring, comparing, revealing, speculating, and most of all theorizing. We will allow them to speak for themselves, but it is worth adding here a little context and explanation.

In October of 2004, the American Folklore Society (AFS) held its annual meeting in Salt Lake City, Utah. Alan Dundes, whose prolific and influential work crossed genres and geographic regions, was asked to give the Invited Presidential Plenary Address. Although he was, as one colleague put it, "the most renowned folklorist of his time" (Hansen 2005, 245), Dundes had not actually participated in the meeting in many years. He delivered, in the words of Regina Bendix,

> one of his rousing, funny, critical, controversial, irreverent, yet erudite papers in the rapid-fire pace in which he tended to lecture—pausing only for an insight, a joke, or an analytic statement to sink in—only to pick up the pace again with more. His address ruffled some feathers, as many of his presentations and publications tended to do; it made the usual demands for rigorous scholarship founded on multilingual bibliographic research and voiced a commitment to an internationally housed discipline; it challenged, politely but firmly, the fieldwork practices of major

scholars in the field; it astonished and purportedly even shocked some younger members of the audience. (Bendix 2005, 485)

The text of Dundes's address, titled "Folkloristics in the Twenty-First Century," was published the following autumn in the *Journal of American Folklore* (Dundes 2005; see also chapter 1), where it continued to provoke controversy and stimulate discussion. Sadly, its impact was made all the more poignant by the fact that the very same issue of the journal contained Dundes's own obituary: he had passed away unexpectedly in the spring of that year, in the months between his oral delivery of the lecture and its publication. In this context his address became, as it were, a provocative parting gesture from the most provocative folklorist of his generation.

Among the many comments in Dundes's paper was a lamentation on the low profile of folkloristics within the academy. "The first, and in my opinion the principal, reason for the decline of folklore programs at universities," he explained, "is the continued lack of innovation in what we might term 'grand theory'" (Dundes 2005, 387; see also chapter 1). This question of *grand theory*—or its lack—was duly taken up at the AFS annual meeting held in October of 2005 when Lee Haring chaired a plenary session featuring a number of prominent folklorists. The panel, titled, "Why Is There No 'Grand Theory' in Folkloristics?" faced these issues head on:

> Does American folkloristics have or need "grand theory"? Can a discipline be taken seriously if it studies culture with no reference to a broader social theory? If past folklore theories have been successively discredited, is there no space for a new one? Where shall folklorists look for a theoretical base? The forum will open such questions; speakers will briefly present their views; much interaction and debate is hoped for. (AFS 2005, 41)

There was indeed "much interaction and debate," and eventually Haring brought together revised versions of the papers presented at that forum, along with a number of others, for a special issue of the *Journal of Folklore Research* (*JFR*) in 2008.

And that special issue has resonated within the discipline. Select articles (and often the entire volume) are assigned in graduate seminars, frequently appear on bibliographies of essential readings in folkloristics, and, of course, on qualifying exams for Masters and Doctoral students. That is to say, the discussion of grand theory—and what it says about American folkloristics, disciplinary histories and futures, and theory in the social sciences more generally—has become required reading for anybody serious about understanding the study of folklore today, particularly as it is practiced and theorized in the United States. Indeed, it should be remembered that the debate on grand theory emerged out of specific concerns within American folkloristic discourse. But that is not to say that it has remained limited to an English-speaking readership: two of the articles, for example, have already been translated and published in leading Japanese folklore journals (Noyes 2011; Bauman 2013).

It is impossible to know what Alan Dundes intended when he delivered that lecture back in 2004. But consummate provocateur that he was, perhaps this continued discussion—and the fact that decades into the twenty-first century students and scholars still grapple with the questions he raised—is exactly what he had in mind. The discourse on grand theory, and especially its exploration in the 2008 issue of *JFR*, continues to compel us to take a long, hard, critical look at folklore studies and ask essential questions about disciplinary definitions, contributions, influences, and responsibilities. And ideally these questions also inspire a more comparative approach to the field, a dynamic international exchange of ideas that encourages folklorists to seek potential answers beyond their own shores.

In his contribution to the *JFR* special issue, Charles Briggs explains that in the 1990s he and Amy Shuman edited a theory-focused special issue of *Western Folklore* (Briggs and Shuman 1993). "But here's the rub," Briggs writes, "Shuman and I attempted to turn these articles into a collection for classroom use, but we were repeatedly told by publishers that there was no market for books on folkloristic theory" (Briggs 2008, 92; see also chapter 12). What then makes it possible for us today to republish the *JFR* issue as a standalone book exploring folkloristic theory and indeed *theorizing* about theory? In part, perhaps, changes in publishing technologies allow us to create a book that can supply the demands of even a relatively specialized market. But more importantly, we are also reaping the compounded benefits of earlier scholarship—of Briggs and Shuman, and many others, to say nothing of the *JFR* special issue itself—that has created an expanding market for theoretically-oriented discussions of folkloristics.

Certainly, though, in this age of JSTOR and Project MUSE, all the individual articles in the 2008 volume are readily available to anybody with access to such databases. But that is just the point: even as the articles are more and more easily accessible, they are increasingly downloaded individually and read as distinct essays. There is no question that they have value and resonance even in this fragmentary form, but at the same time they become utterances extracted from a more complex conversation. One objective of the present book is, in a sense, to rechristen these articles as chapters, to put the individual essays back into conversation with each other and allow them to resonate, sometimes harmoniously and sometimes in productive cacophony. To make an analogy to music, it goes without saying that "With a Little Help from My Friends" and "Lucy in the Sky with Diamonds" are classics that invite repeated listening. But when we play the *Sgt. Pepper's Lonely Hearts Club Band* album as a whole, each of its component songs is heard differently, as part of a larger performance, with more depth and complexity. Moreover, on a practical level, we hope that this coherent collection of chapters will be suitable (in content as well as length) for classroom use. And ideally, the discussion in the folklore seminar room will also entice scholars from related fields—such as cultural studies, anthropology, ethnomusicology, and media studies—to join the conversation.

With this recontextualization in mind, the present volume consists of all the original essays published in the 2008 *JFR* special issue. In addition, we set the stage with a reprint of Dundes's address from the *Journal of American Folklore* (2005). We have also added a new essay, a brief personal narrative from Chad Buterbaugh, a recent PhD in folklore from Indiana University. Buterbaugh reflects on his own experiences studying (that is, being assigned) the 2008 *JFR* special issue and how the text has helped shape understandings of the discipline for his own emerging generation of professional folklorists. And finally, Lee Haring has contributed a brief afterword as well, reassessing the project a decade after its inception, and looking toward the future. Our objective in framing the issue in this way, with a new beginning and a new end, is not to seal off the discourse, but just the opposite: to remember that the conversation is ongoing and open-ended (on both ends), and to encourage new thinking and fresh theorization.

Many people made this book project a reality. First and foremost, of course, none of this would have been possible if Lee Haring had not organized the AFS conference session and edited the original *JFR* issue. Likewise, profound gratitude must go to Moira Marsh, editor of *JFR* at that time. We also thank Diane E. Goldstein for pointing out to us that her own copy of the original *JFR* issue was falling apart after many years of use and suggesting that it would be a good candidate for the *Encounters* book series. With Indiana University Press we are fortunate to have a publisher able to combine technological know-how with a passion for folklore studies and the prescience to recognize the value of publishing this work in a book format; we are most grateful to Gary Dunham and Michael Regoli who enthusiastically embraced this idea and pushed it forward to fruition. We would also like to thank Rachel Kindler for her editorial assistance on this edited volume. We thank the American Folklore Society and the *Journal of American Folklore* for generously allowing us to republish "Folkloristics in the Twenty-First Century."

Michael Dylan Foster
Ray Cashman
Series Editors, *Encounters: Explorations in Folklore and Ethnomusicology*

References

American Folklore Society. 2005. *Annual Meeting, Program and Abstracts: Folklore, Equal Access and Social Justice.*

Bendix, Regina. 2005. "Alan Dundes (1934–2005)." *Journal of American Folklore* 118 (470): 485–488.

Bauman, Richard. 2013. "Vuanakyuraa no bunkengaku." Translated by Taniguchi Yōko. *Nihon minzokugaku* 273 (February): 9–16.

Briggs, Charles L. 2008. "Disciplining Folklorists." *Journal of Folklore Research* 45 (1) (January–April): 91–105.

Briggs, Charles L. and Amy Shuman, ed. 1993. *Theorizing Folklore.* (Special Issue) *Western Folklore* 52 (2–3): 3–4.

Dundes, Alan. 2005. "Folkloristics in the Twenty-First Century (AFS Invited Presidential Plenary Address, 2004)." *Journal of American Folklore* 118 (470): 385–408.

Hansen, William. 2005. "Alan Dundes 1934–2005." *Journal of Folklore Research* 42 (2): 245–250.

Noyes, Dorothy. 2011. "Hanburu seorii." Translated by Oikawa Takashi. *Gendai minzokugaku kenkyū* 3: 71–79.

Grand Theory in Folkloristics

The Provocation

1 Folkloristics in the Twenty-First Century*

THE STATE OF folkloristics at the beginning of the twenty-first century is depressingly worrisome. Graduate programs in folklore around the world have been disestablished or seriously weakened. The once-celebrated program at the University of Copenhagen no longer exists. Folklore programs in Germany have changed their title in an effort to become ethnology-centered (Korff 1996). Even in Helsinki, the veritable Mecca of folklore research, the name of the graduate program at the University of Helsinki has been changed. According to the website, "The Department of Folklore Studies, along with the departments of Ethnology, Cultural Anthropology and Archaeology, belongs administratively to the Faculty of Arts and the Institute of Cultural Research." The latter title sounds suspiciously like "cultural studies" to me, and cultural studies consists of literary types who would like to be cultural anthropologists. I hate to think of folklorists being grouped with such wannabes! Here in the United States, the situation is even worse. UCLA's doctoral program in folklore and mythology has been subsumed under the rubric of World Arts and Cultures, and the folklore doctorate has been reduced to one of several options in that expansion of what was formerly a department of dance. The doctoral program in folklore and folklife at the University of Pennsylvania has virtually collapsed and may not recover unless there is an infusion of new faculty members. Even Indiana University, the acknowledged

* American Folklore Society invited Presidential Plenary Address, 2004. From the *Journal of American Folklore.* Copyright 2005 by the Board of Trustees of the University of Illinois. Used with permission of the University of Illinois Press. Originally published as Alan Dundes, "Folkloristics in the Twenty-First Century (AFS Invited Presidential Plenary Address)," *Journal of American Folklore* 118, no. 470 (Fall 2005): 385–408.

bastion and beacon of folklore study in the United States, has seen fit to combine folklore with ethnomusicology into one administrative unit. As a result, there is no longer a purely separate, independent doctoral program in folklore per se anywhere in the United States, a sad situation in my view.

Some may feel that these administrative shifts are nothing more than a reflection of the name-changing discussion arising from those among you who have expressed unhappiness with the term "folklore" as the name of our discipline. Regina Bendix was quite right when she made the astute observation that the very coining of the term "folklore" by William Thoms was itself a case of name changing (from "popular antiquities," the Latinate construction, to the Anglo-Saxon "folklore"; 1998, 235). However, I believe she was sadly mistaken when she claimed that part of the disrepute of the field was caused by using the same term "folklore" for both the subject matter and the name of the discipline. This is, in my opinion, a red herring, a nonproblem that was perfectly well solved by several nineteenth-century folklorists, including Reinhold Köhler (1887), who distinguished between "folklore," the subject matter, and "folkloristics," the study of that subject matter. The term "folkloristics" goes back to the 1880s at the very least. In 1996, Eric Montenyohl informed us, "Of course the term 'folkloristics' is quite modern in comparison to 'folklore.' The distinction between the discipline and the subject material and the appropriate term for each came into discussion in the 1980s. Until that time, folklore referred to both the subject and the discipline which studied it—one more reason for confusion" (1996, 234n2). Montenyohl probably is referring to Bruce Jackson's equally uninformed note in *JAF* in 1985 in which Jackson complains about the term "folkloristics" and proposes that it be banned, as if anyone could possibly legislate language usage. Jackson quotes Roger Abrahams's claim that I invented the term as a joke. I certainly did not. On December 7, 1889, American folklorist Charles G. Leland (1834–1903), in an address greeting the newly formed Hungarian Folklore Society, spoke of "Die Folkloristik" as one of the most profound developments in history (Leland 1890–1892). So folkloristics is the study of folklore just as linguistics is the study of language, and it has been for more than a century, even if parochial American folklorists are not aware of the fact. Yuriy Sokolov's textbook *Russian Folklore,* first published in 1938, recognizes the distinction, and the valuable first chapter of the book is titled

"The Nature of Folklore and the Problems of Folkloristics." The Sokolov usage was pointed out by Barbara Kirshenblatt-Gimblett in her rebuttal note "Di folkloristik: A Good Yiddish Word," also in *JAF* (1985). She also remarked that Åke Hultkrantz, in his important *General Ethnological Concepts* (1960), used "folkloristik" as a synonym for "the science of folklore." The distinction between folklore and folkloristics, therefore, is hardly a new idea, and I stated or, if you like, "re-stated" it as clearly as I could in my prefatory "What Is Folklore" in the edited volume *The Study of Folklore* (1965). I regret that neither Dan Ben-Amos nor Elliott Oring reiterated this important distinction between folkloristics and folklore in their otherwise excellent, spirited defense of the discipline in their respective 1998 essays in *JAF*. But in contrast, I was pleased that Robert Georges and Michael Owen Jones titled their useful textbook *Folkloristics: An Introduction,* and they stress the distinction between "folklore" and "folkloristics" on the very first page (1985). Jan Harold Brunvand did not include the term in the first edition of his mainstream textbook, *The Study of American Folklore,* which first appeared in 1968, but by the second edition (1978) he decided to include the term on the first page of the book and it has remained in later editions (1986, 1998) as referring to "the study of folklore," but he insisted on placing the term in quotation marks, which suggests he was not altogether comfortable with it. I have, however, noted the increasing usage of the term "folkloristics" in recent scholarship, and I believe it bodes well.

I am not suggesting that we change the name of the American Folklore Society to Folkloristics Society of America to parallel the Linguistics Society of America. Rather, the critical question remaining is rather why folkloristics, the academic study of folklore, a subject that should be part of every major university and college curricular offerings, is in such obvious decline. Another related sad sign is the unfortunate demise of the journal *Southern Folklore,* the successor to the older *Southern Folklore Quarterly.* This was once a major folklore periodical in the United States, and I keep hoping that an enterprising folklorist at one of our many great southern colleges or universities will resuscitate this journal. I think there are reasons for the decline, and I also think some of the responsibility for the decline lies in part with the membership of the American Folklore Society (myself included). I suspect that some of you may think that I may have endorsed the scandalously discouraging essay that appeared in *Lingua Franca* in

October of 1997 that made the dire prediction that "folklore as an autonomous discipline at Penn may well be doomed" (Dorfman 1997, 8). This essay that proclaimed the discipline of folkloristics as moribund, if not actually deceased, was all the more insulting because it was titled "That's All Folks!" which is a borrowing from popular culture, namely, the "Looney Tunes" and "Merrie Melodies" Bugs Bunny tradition. These words uttered by a stuttering Porky Pig signified that the cartoon was over. (Incidentally the use of a stuttering pig, and other insults to individuals with various speech impediments and other disabilities, would no longer be deemed politically correct.) But the use of the tag line as a title of the article essentially equates the field of folklore to an animated cartoon that is over. I am not aware that any folklorist wrote a letter of protest or rebuttal, although I tried to do so. (I am sorry to say my response, "Folkloristics Redivivus," was not published by *Lingua Franca*, though it does appear on the journal's website (www.temple.edu/isllc/newfolk/dundes2.html). The last paragraph of my response reads, "At a moment in American history when multicultural diversity is being celebrated, this is precisely when enlightened university administrators ought to be encouraging practitioners of an international discipline which goes back to Herder and the Grimms, a discipline which has been ahead of its time in recognizing the importance of folklore in promoting ethnic pride and in providing invaluable data for the discovery of native cognitive categories and patterns of worldview and values." *Lingua Franca* did publish several short letters of protest, including one from Indiana University titled "Is Folklore Finished?" but it was signed by Liz Locke and eighty other graduate students. Nothing from the Indiana faculty. No letter from the IU faculty and no letter of protest from AFS. Not a peep! It seems to me that both academic and public sector folklorists have a stake in defending our discipline when it is attacked. Where was the AFS leadership on this occasion? Is it a case of the proverb "Silence gives consent"? Did, or does, AFS think that folklore as a discipline is dead? I might add parenthetically, and perhaps a little gleefully, that *Lingua Franca*, which started in 1991, ended in 2001; so it turned out that, after all, it was *Lingua Franca* and not folklore that died a premature death; and I can happily report that the study of folklore successfully defied its gloomy prophecy and lives on.

The first, and in my opinion the principal, reason for the decline of folklore programs at universities is the continued lack of innovation in what we might term "grand theory." In *Lingua Franca* parlance, "Folklore is considered undertheorized." Elliott Oring, one of our few folklore theorists, put it equally succinctly as an aside in his article "On the Future of American Folklore Studies: A Response": "Folklore is liminal precisely because it has no theory or methodology that governs its perspective" (1991, 80). Any academic discipline worth its salt must have basic theoretical and methodological concepts. Folkloristics has some, to be sure, but most of them were devised in the nineteenth or early twentieth century and have been neither superseded nor supplemented. Interestingly enough, most grand theory in folklore was proposed by armchair or library folklorists, not fieldworkers. I am thinking of Sir James Frazer's formulation of the principles of sympathetic magic or Max Müller's speculations about solar mythology. Even in the twentieth century, what little grand theory does exist comes from Sigmund Freud and Claude Lévi-Strauss, neither of whom would qualify as fieldworkers. Most fieldworkers, on the contrary, are involved with local communities and are not always concerned with the theoretical implications of the data they gather.

Historically speaking, the roots of the discipline of folkloristics lie in antiquarianism, or what I might term as the quest for the quaint or perhaps the quest for the curious. In my travels to folklore centers overseas and in this country, I see more often than not what I would call "butterfly collecting." Items of folklore are treated as rare exotica, metaphorically speaking, to have a pin stuck through them and mounted in a display archival case such that it is almost impossible to imagine the folklore items were ever alive (that is, performed). Context is typically ignored, and it is the text only that is prized by the local collector. Because such local collectors who ought to have ideas of a theoretical or methodological nature do not, the field has by default been left to armchair library scholars, the modern analogues to Frazer. In the United States, the atheoretical void is exacerbated by the paucity of even armchair or library scholars. Despite the richness of our library resources and the infinite capacity of information technology with its dazzling array of databases, American folklorists have contributed precious little to folklore theory and method. Almost every viable theoretical and methodological concept employed in folkloristics has come from Europe. In one sense, I suppose it doesn't really matter where a good idea comes from. Folkloristics is and always has been an international discipline. So we gladly use

French folklorist Arnold Van Gennep's notion of "rites of passage," Finnish folklorist Kaarle Krohn's "historic-geographic method," or Swedish folklorist Carl Wilhelm von Sydow's concepts of "active bearer" and "oicotype." But all these concepts were formulated at the end of the nineteenth century or early twentieth century. Where are the new hypotheses and speculations about folklore?

Now, I can just imagine that some of you folklorists, especially those imbued with a healthy dose of nationalism and pride, are saying to yourselves, "Wait a minute. Americans have made contributions to theoretical folkloristics. What about feminist theory? What about performance theory? What about oral formulaic theory?" Well, what about these so-called theories? Although Milman Parry and Albert Lord are given credit for developing oral formulaic theory, John Foley has shown that the roots of the theory came from European scholars who preceded them (1988, 7–15). The situation is analogous to Francis Child's canonical collection of English and Scottish ballads, which was incontestably modeled after the Danish folklorist Svend Grundtvig's massive treatment of Danish ballads or Stith Thompson's revision of Finnish folklorist Antti Aarne's tale type index. American folklorists have, for the most part, been followers, not leaders. I have to admit that I fall into this category myself, having been inspired by Russian folklorist Vladimir Propp's *Morphology of the Folktale* (1968) and Austrian Sigmund Freud's psychoanalytic theory.

As for feminist theory, what precisely is the "theory" in feminist theory? Despite the existence of books and articles with "feminist theory" in their titles, one looks in vain for a serious articulation of what that "theory" is. The idea that women's voices and women's roles in society have been adversely impacted by male chauvinism and bias is certainly true, but does that truism constitute a proper "theory"? And what of "performance theory"? No folklorist would deny that folklore lives only when it is performed, that folklore performances involve participants and audiences, and that the issue of competence in performance is a feature to be recorded and analyzed, but where is the "theory" in performance theory? I do not consider either so-called feminist theory or performance theory to be "grand theory." As far as I'm concerned, they are simply pretentious ways of saying that we should study folklore as performed, and we should be more sensitive to the depiction of women in folkloristic texts and contexts.

True grand theories allow us to understand data that would otherwise remain enigmatic, if not indecipherable. Here we may observe that some of the older grand theories continue to yield insight. Consider the Jewish superstition that one should never have a button sewed on or a garment otherwise repaired while a person is wearing that garment. Informants, if asked, can shed little light on the possible rationale underlying the belief. But with the help of Frazer's law of homeopathic magic, we can quite easily explain the custom. The only time a garment is sewed while it is worn is when a corpse is being dressed for burial. Hence, sewing on a detached button or repairing a tear in a garment is treating the wearer of the garment as a corpse and, in effect, signifying or forecasting that the individual might soon die. No wonder it is considered to be such a taboo.

In maritime folklore, we learn that it is bad luck to whistle while on board ship. I can remember back in my own days in the United States Navy being chastised by a warrant officer for whistling. Why should whistling be forbidden on a ship? Once again, grand theory can help us. Whistling, given the principle of "like produces like," the basis of Frazer's law of homeopathic magic, is a model of a windstorm. There is even a folk metaphor "to whistle up a storm." Although wind was clearly a necessity in days of sail, too much wind was not a desideratum as it might result in a ship's capsizing and sinking. The point here is that grand theory, once formulated, may continue to yield insight.

As many of you know, I find that psychoanalytic theory qualifies as grand theory, allowing us to fathom otherwise inexplicable folkloristic data. For example, there is a Japanese superstition that "pregnant women should never open an oven door." Informants could say only that it was bad luck. But with the knowledge gained from the symbolic equivalence of oven and womb (as attested in the phrase even in American folklore that a pregnant woman "has a bun in the oven"), we can understand that this is once again an application of Frazer's homeopathic magic. Opening an oven door would be an invitation for a miscarriage to occur. In this case, we have to use both Freud and Frazer to fully explain this superstition. The point is that most collections of superstitions, like the majority of folklore collections—be they proverbs or folktales—offer no explanation whatsoever. Let me give one further illustration of the application of psychoanalytic theory to a puzzling item of folklore.

From medieval Spain to modern-day Latin America, one of the most popular Spanish ballads is known as "Delgadina." More than 500 versions of this romance-corrido have been published. Famed Spanish ballad scholar Ramón Menéndez Pidal claimed that this Spanish ballad "is found wherever the Spanish language is spoken" (Herrera-Sobek 1986, 91) and expressed his belief that "'Delgadina' is without a doubt the most widely known romance in Spain and America" (106n 11). The summary of the ballad: "'Delgadina' tells the story of a young woman who resists her father's incestuous advances. For this, she is locked up and denied anything to drink while she is fed only salty foods" (Mariscal Hay 2002, 20; Goldberg 2000, 148, Motif T411.1 Father desires daughter sexually. She refuses.). The abundant scholarship on the ballad tends to treat it as a literal reflection of the horrors of father-daughter incest and, in particular, of the absolute power of the father in the Hispanic family structure (Herrera-Sobek 1986), but no one to date has offered a convincing explanation of just why this ballad has enjoyed so many centuries of popularity. Delgadina is the youngest of three daughters of the king, and in some versions she wears provocative clothing, including a "transparent dress." In many versions of the ballad, there is some dispute over who is to blame for the father's attempt to make Delgadina his mistress. Often it is Delgadina who is blamed by her sisters or her mother. In one verse, after Delgadina begs her mother in vain for a jug of water, the mother responds, "Get away Delgadina, get away you evil bitch / because of you here I am seven years a wronged wife." In another version, a Sephardic one (Aitken 1928, 46), the mother replies, "Get thee thence, Jewish beast! Get thee down, cruel beast: On thy account these seven years I have lived unhappy in marriage." It is important to note that this ballad is typically sung by women to other women (Egan 1996). Thus, it is clearly very much a women's song (Aitken 1928). The daughter fantasizes that her father is not happy with her mother but would prefer her instead. As Aitken puts it in her 1928 article, the girl is jealous of her mother and thinks, "My father really prefers me to my mother and would like to put me in her place and over my elder sisters" (1928, 48).

In a parallel (cognate) ballad (of Silvana), it is arranged that the mother takes the daughter's place in bed for the prearranged meeting with the father-king (Goldberg 2000, 100, Motif Q260.1). What I believe we have with this version, what Wendy Doniger refers to as the "bedtrick" (2000), is what I have termed "projective inversion" (Dundes 1976, 2002). If we perceive this celebrated ballad as a thinly disguised Electral story, we can see that it represents wishful thinking on the part of the daughter. She loves her father and wants to replace her mother in the marital bed. This taboo wish is transformed via projection into the father's attempt to seduce his daughter. The mother's substituting for the daughter in the parental bed is a perfect inversion of the taboo wish. Instead of the daughter substituting for her mother, the mother substitutes for the daughter, thereby saving the daughter from a taboo incestuous sexual act. The specific reference to the daughter being fed salt cannot help but remind us of AT 923, "Love like Salt" (the basis of the King Lear plot), which also involves a king-father's attempt to have incestuous relations with his daughter. This plot is also reminiscent of AT 706, "The Maiden without Hands," which occurs in ballad form (Brewster 1972, 11–12) and has also been interpreted by me as a striking case of projective inversion (Dundes 1987). One could also mention the tale of Lot's wife, who is turned to salt, after which his daughters seduce their drunken father, a quite explicit Electral tale.

Whether one agrees with these interpretations or not, one can certainly see that the interpretations would not have been possible without recourse to grand theory, in this case, Freud's Oedipal theory and my modest addition of the concept of projective inversion. As for the reasons for the long-lived popularity of a father-daughter incest projection in Hispanic cultures, it is worth remembering that the central plot of Catholicism involves a virgin being impregnated without her consent by a heavenly father, another Electral fantasy with overtones of projective inversion. In summary form, "I would like to seduce my father but that is forbidden, so in the projection it is my father who seduces me, much to my mother's consternation, with the psychological advantage of leaving me guilt-free. It's not my fault that my father desires me." The popularity of this plot in Catholic circles is also attested by the legend of Saint Dymphna. After her mother died, her father, a pagan Irish chieftain named Damon, searched the whole world for a woman to replace his wife but was unsuccessful until he returned home and saw that his daughter Dymphna was as beautiful as her mother. He makes advances, but she flees. He catches up with her in Belgium, but when she refuses to surrender, he kills her. The fact that the daughter dies or has her masturbatory hands cut off (in AT 706) is a sign that it is, in the final analysis, she who is ultimately being punished for her original incestuous wish. Now, admittedly, this particular type of grand theory is not widely accepted by conventional mainstream folklorists, but my point is that, without this or other grand theories, folklore texts will forever remain as mere collectanea with little or no substantive content analysis. The stereotype of folklorists as simply collectors, obsessive classifiers, and archivists is strengthened each and every time yet another collection of unanalyzed folklore is published.

And this brings me to the second major reason for the decline of folkloristics as a respected and honored academic discipline. One reason, as I have noted, is the lack of new grand theory, but a second reason, I believe, is that we professional folklorists are badly outnumbered by amateurs who give our field a bad name. In the first week of June 2004, I was invited to participate in an ambitious conference in Atlanta called "Mythic Journeys," designed to honor the centennial of the birth of Joseph Campbell. The event was organized by the Mythic Imagination Institute, supported by the Joseph Campbell Foundation and the Jung Society of Atlanta, and sponsored by a number of groups and corporations, including Borders Books and Music, *Parabola Magazine,* and the Krispy Kreme Foundation. Although there were dozens of panels and presentations that were concerned with folklore (though not necessarily myth), there were very few professional folklorists in attendance. The presenters included storytellers, artists, filmmakers, Jungian analytical psychologists, and a very few individuals who were self-identified as folklorists. Before leaving for Atlanta, out of curiosity I looked up a number of my fellow panelists and presenters and was quite startled to discover that many of them were faculty members at small colleges who were listed as professors of folklore and who obviously taught courses in what they termed "folklore." The courses were typically concerned with searching for Jungian archetypes in literature, including J. R. R. Tolkien, or exploring manifestations of Campbell's composite "monomyth" that has little if anything to do with myth proper but is, rather, based on a combination of legend and folktale. Now there is no way other than establishing a fascist police state for the American Folklore Society to prevent such "folklorists" from teaching what they call "folklore." Robert Georges wrote an essay indicating his disgust at discovering

that there are many individuals who simply declare themselves to
be folklorists without any formal training or study of the subject
(1991, 3–4). Can one possibly imagine anyone claiming to be a physi-
cist or mathematician without ever having had formal training in
physics or mathematics? Georges also expressed disappointment that
many who are trained as folklorists conceal that fact, preferring instead to claim that they belong to other academic disciplines. Here I
cannot forbear reminding you of one of the worst recorded instances
of a folklorist refusing to acknowledge his disciplinary affiliation. It
happened in 1992 at UCLA. Exiled president of Haiti, Jean-Bertrand
Aristide, who has an interest in folklore, was scheduled to speak on
campus. Donald Cosentino was at that time the chair of the folklore
and mythology program. As is customary on such occasions, a high-
ranking official was on the stage to welcome the audience before
turning the gavel over to Cosentino to introduce the speaker. Right
before the event began, the UCLA vice-chancellor whispered to
Cosentino, "We have a head of state here. Under no circumstances
will I introduce you as the chair of folklore and mythology. I will
introduce you as from the English department. Let's not embarrass
ourselves." Cosentino did as instructed and introduced Aristide
without identifying himself as chair of the folklore and mythology
program. What bothers me most about this incident is not so much
the vice-chancellor's outrageous insult to our field, but the fact that
Cosentino did not fight it, instead cowardly acquiescing. I can assure
you that had I been in such a position, short of punching out the vice-
chancellor publicly on stage, I would have actually reported his whispered conversation and proudly announced my position as chair of
folklore and mythology. In other words, I would have sought to embarrass the vice-chancellor rather than have him embarrass me and
my field. A truly disgraceful incident in our academic history, one that
was the very first item mentioned in the *Lingua Franca* attack
(Dorfman 1997).

    Related to the fact that we seem to be besieged by popularizer
nonfolklorists masquerading as folklore scholars, if one walks into
any of the large commercial bookstores such as Barnes and Noble or
Borders and checks the "folklore and mythology" sections, what does
one find? There are the inevitable numerous anthologies of Greek
myths or dictionaries of mythology containing mostly entries devoted
to Greek and Roman mythology, volumes of folktales from all over

the world *retold* by editors—the word "retold" should be anathema to professional folklorists—typically bowdlerized and dumbed-down for children, and finally, at least a half dozen books by Joseph Campbell. I recall one incident several years ago in the Barnes and Noble bookstore in Berkeley. Although I much prefer secondhand bookstores, occasionally I check the commercial stores just to see if there is a new book that I should know about. On this occasion, I found myself unable to locate the folklore and mythology section. It had evidently been moved, as bookstores often reshuffle shelves and sections. I finally went to one of the bookstore personnel to be directed to the folklore and mythology section. Normally in such bookstores, sections are clearly labeled: religion, sociology, self-help, and so forth. In this case, the folklore and mythology label was absent and in its place was simply emblazoned in large bold letters: "Joseph Campbell." I was shocked to discover that the entire folklore and mythology section had been subsumed under Campbell's name. I remember being almost relieved that at least none of my books were to be found in that section. My sole point in mentioning this disheartening incident is to suggest that for many members of the literate public, the study of folklore means precisely Campbell and his writings. Yet professional folklorists have said very little about the huge corpus of Campbelliana. I do not know if any of his many books were ever even reviewed in *JAF*. Is this a case of "silence gives assent"? Very likely more people were introduced to the subject matter of folklore by the writings of Campbell or the PBS television series of lectures by him than by any other source. And yet we folklorists have said little or nothing about him and his theories.

My thesis is simply this: the combination of a lack of new grand theory and the failure to counter the effective efforts of numerous amateurs and dilettantes who have successfully claimed possession of the field of folklore as their fiefdom has understandably led to a public perception of folkloristics as a weak academic discipline, a perception unfortunately too often shared by college and university administrators. The American Folklore Society, since its inception, has had as its goal the professionalization of the discipline of folk-loristics. *JAF* should be the primary forum for the expression of new theoretical and methodological advances and the book review section of the journal should critique and rebut amateurish attempts to analyze folkloristic data. I am not blaming the past or present editors of *JAF* for the failure to do so. They can only publish articles submitted to them by us folklorists constituting the membership of AFS. So we must accept the blame for the state of our discipline. And, accordingly, it is up to us to fulfill the promise of our beloved field to demonstrate to all interested parties that folkloristics is a world-class global discipline with its own valid theories and methods, and we should not leave our field by default to popularizers and amateurs. Fakelore and folklorismus abound everywhere, and we run the risk of being overwhelmed by the sheer quantity of unscholarly anthologies of adulterated folklore mixed with creative writing.

At the Mythic Journeys conference held in June in Atlanta, there was a splendid associated website with stunningly brilliant graphics. On the screen appeared a map of the world and one could click on different areas (peoples) and a myth from that area/people would appear accompanied by a sonorous narration of it. Very impressive indeed! But at the bottom of the screen there were various alternative options. One of the options was "write your own myth." I saw at one point that a number of ten- and eleven-year-old children had accepted the challenge and had e-mailed "their own myths" to the website. Nothing irritates me more than when, after I give a lecture on folklore to a group of elementary or secondary school teachers, one enthusiastic teacher comes up afterward to say that she very much appreciates the importance of myth and that is why she encourages her second-grade class to write myths as an exercise. No wonder such children eventually grow up to be confused about what myths really are and to become fans of Campbell's contention that all of us can be heroes of our own myths.

As apparently no folklorist has hitherto made any critique of Campbell, I should like to take this opportunity to do so. Part of the problem stems from the fact that Campbell does not really know what a myth is, and he does not really distinguish it from folktale and legend, two genres that provide most of the illustrative examples in his popular *Hero with a Thousand Faces,* first published in 1949. His illustrative examples include Little Red Riding Hood and the Porcupine subtype of Star Husband, neither of which any folklorist would dream of classifying as myth. Campbell tries to delineate a worldwide hero pattern, but he makes no mention of J. G. von Hahn's initial pioneering statement of 1876 in which he sought to isolate features of what he termed the Aryan Expulsion and Return hero pattern (Segal 1990, vii). Nor does Campbell refer to Otto Rank's path-breaking *Myth of the Birth of the Hero* first published in 1909 or Lord Raglan's famous pattern of the hero biography which appeared as an article in *Folklore* in 1934 and shortly thereafter in book form in 1936 (see Dundes 1965).

Let me say something more about *The Hero with a Thousand Faces*, still Campbell's best-known book, and his first. Where did he get that resonant catchy title? In 1940, Campbell met Swami Nikhilananda (Larsen and Larsen 1993, 283), who was a devoted disciple of Ramakrishna. In *The Hero with a Thousand Faces*, Campbell cites Swami Nikhilananda's translation of *The Gospel of Sri Ramakrishna* (Campbell [1949] 1956, 115n 33). We know that Campbell was very intrigued by the writings of Sri Ramakrishna (Larsen and Larsen 1993, 283–86). In the second volume of *The Cultural Heritage of India*, the Sri Ramakrisna Centenary Memorial, Swami Nikhilananda contributed a 176-page essay titled "Sri Ramakrishna and Spiritual Renaissance" (1936, 441–617). We know that Campbell read the 1936 essay because he cited it in his 1960 essay, "Primitive Man as Metaphysician." Consider the following quote from Ramakrishna contained in Nikhilananda's essay: "But he who is called Krishna is also called Shiva and bears the names Shakti, Jesus, and Allah as well—*the one Rama with a thousand names*... The substance is one under different names" (1936; emphasis added). We know that Campbell was a truly voracious reader and a master of assimilating much of what he read. We shall never know for certain, but the passage bears an eerie resemblance to Campbell's title. We have only to substitute "hero" for "Rama" and "faces" for "names" and we get "the one hero with a thousand faces." Note, I am arguing inspiration here, not plagiarism. In any case, the Campbell classic has been called "a sweeping and engrossing study of the hero myth" (Ellwood 1999, 143). But the narratives analyzed by Campbell are not myths at all; they are folktales and legends.

In his discussion of "The Magic Flight," which is strictly a folktale motif, Campbell includes the narrative of Jason's quest for the Golden Fleece ([1949] 1956, 203–204), but this has nothing whatever to do with myth proper. Rather it is a hero legend. There is nothing in the narrative referring to the creation of the world or humankind. In view of Campbell's abiding interest in the "quest" theme, it is not surprising that he frequently cites Arthurian material ([1949]

1956, 330), a subject he studied for his master's thesis at Columbia University (Larsen and Larsen 1991, 75), including mention of the search for the Holy Grail. But such Arthurian stories are definitely legends, not myths. In *Creative Mythology,* the fourth volume of Campbell's tetralogy *The Masks of God,* he retells Gottfried von Strassburg's *Tristan* and Wolfram von Eschenbach's *Parzifal.* These are significant major medieval literary masterpieces, but by no stretch of the folkloristic imagination could either one be considered a myth. Campbell suggests that Wolfram utilized "an altogether secular mythology" (1968, 476), but myth is sacred, not secular. At best these texts might be construed as literary legends. Yet both involve quests specifically associated with the Holy Grail. Campbell also considers Thomas Mann and James Joyce as mythmakers. One can only conclude that *Creative Mythology* does not deal with "myth" in the strict technical sense at all. Rather, it is a volume of essentially wide-ranging literary criticism. Considering that Campbell is not clear about what a myth is, no wonder his myriad followers are equally confused. This loose definition of "myth," one unfortunately shared by many writers on the subject, would seem to confirm Gregory Hansen's criticism that definitions of folklore (and that would include myth) have been stretched so far as to include everything. Some writers of books on myths include "B" movies and novels under the rubric of myth. As Hansen words it, "The problem is that if everything is now 'folklore,' then nothing is 'folklore'" (1997, 99).

Campbell's adaptation of folklorist Van Gennep's rites of passage pattern, applied to narratives, was certainly insightful, but the universalist assumption based on an unproven assumption of psychic unity—namely, that all peoples possess the same mythic structure—is not. In *Creative Mythology,* the fourth volume of the teratology *The Masks of God,* Campbell himself refers to *The Hero* as follows: "In *The Hero with a Thousand Faces* I have shown that myths and wonder tales . . . belong to a general type which I have called 'The Adventure of the Hero,' that has not changed in essential form through the documented history of mankind" (1968, 480).

It has long been a popular fantasy among amateur students of myth that all peoples share the same stories. This is clearly an example of wishful thinking. Campbell referred to the hero pattern as a universal monomyth, borrowing this vacuous portmanteau neologism from Joyce's *Finnegan's Wake* (Campbell [1949] 1956, 30n 35).

On the universality issue, the empirical facts suggest otherwise. There is not one single myth that is universal, a statement that runs counter to Campbell's view. He was invited to contribute to a special issue of *Daedalus* devoted to "Myth and Mythmaking" in 1959, an issue that also contained contributions by Mircea Eliade, Clyde Kluckhohn, and Richard Dorson. Campbell began his essay, "The Historical Development of Mythology," which was based on his introduction to his then forthcoming *Masks of God* series, with the following statement: "The comparative study of the mythologies of the world compels us to view the cultural history of mankind as a unit; for we find that such themes as the Fire-theft, Deluge, Land of the Dead, Virgin Birth, and Resurrected Hero have a world-wide distribution, appearing everywhere in new combinations, while remaining, like the elements of a kaleidoscope, only a few and *always the same*" (1959, 232; emphasis added). Even a beginning student of folklore could dispute this kind of argument by assertion. It is easy to make ex cathedra pronouncements about universals, but it is quite difficult to document them. Take the virgin birth, for example. If we look in the Motif-Index, we find Motif T547, Birth from Virgin, with just three citations listed for the motif. One refers to European saints, another to a classical Greek myth, and one to a South American Indian source. Period. I am not aware of any virgin birth stories in Africa. None are cited in the Motif-Index for Siberia, Polynesia, or Melanesia. We have dozens of myths reported from aboriginal Australia and New Guinea, but evidently no virgin birth stories there. So can we accept Campbell's assertion on faith that the virgin birth has a worldwide distribution? In *The Hero with a Thousand Faces*, Campbell has a whole section devoted to the virgin birth ([1949] 1956, 297–314), but the one African text cited tells of the first man having intercourse with his wives and daughters to produce children and animals, hardly a convincing example of a virgin birth. In his list of universals, Campbell also mentions the deluge. In my edited volume, *The Flood Myth*, one can easily ascertain that this myth is essentially absent from sub-Saharan Africa (1988).

Campbell plays fast and loose with folklore data to illustrate his so-called hero pattern. For example, in the section titled "The Belly of the Whale," Campbell cites the story of Jonah, and I am sure that western ethnocentric readers nod their head in approval as this narrative of the Old Testament would seem to be a perfect example of this theme (though technically the creature is not really identified as a whale). Campbell then goes on to cite as a second illustrative example "The little German girl, Red Riding Hood, was swallowed by a wolf" ([1949] 1956, 91). This narrative, of course, is not a myth, but a folktale, namely Aarne-Thompson Tale Type 333, about a girl, which makes it about a heroine, not a hero. Does Campbell's pattern apply equally to the female of the species or only to males (cf. Lefkowitz 1990, 430)? And the alleged swallower is not a whale but a wolf. But, more important, we know that, in the oral version of this girl-centered folktale (as opposed to the literary rewritings by males such as Charles Perrault and the Brothers Grimm), the girl is not swallowed by the wolf at all. Instead she escapes through a clever ruse by pretending to need to go outside to defecate. So because Red Riding Hood is a heroine, not a hero, and because she was not swallowed by the wolf (or tigress in the Korean, Japanese, and Chinese versions), it would seem, then, that this tale is not really the best possible evidence for the existence of an element of a supposed universal mythic pattern titled "In the Belly of the Whale."

Despite the lack of evidence, Campbell appears to have no doubt about the existence of folklore universals. In this respect, he is a throwback to nineteenth-century theories of psychic unity. Most folklorists would agree that the occurrence of parallels is due to monogenesis and diffusion rather than polygenesis, but this is not Campbell's position. His method, if we can even bear to call it such, is largely based on Adolf Bastian's unsubstantiated notion of "Elementargedanke," or elementary ideas, a clear-cut intellectual precursor to Carl Jung's concept of archetype, both of which are uncritically adopted by Campbell (1972, 44; 1968, 653; Campbell and Toms 1990, 68). In his "Bios and Mythos: Prolegomena to a Science of Mythology," written for Géza Rûheim's 1951 festschrift, Campbell makes this unequivocal statement: "However, it is of first importance not to lose sight of the fact that the mythological archetypes (Bastian's Elementary Ideas) cut across the boundaries of . . . culture spheres and are not confined to any one or two, but are variously represented in all" (1951, 333). Campbell eventually, by his own admission, came to prefer Jung to Freud, although he used both in *The Hero with a Thousand Faces* (Campbell and Toms 1990, 121). And he seems to have accepted the idea of Jung's "collective unconscious." "Mythology," according to Campbell, "is the expression of the collective unconscious." In marked contrast to Jung, however, he does occasionally accept the fact that diffusion can account for the occurrence of cross-cultural correspondences in myths (1990, 123).

Still, it is Campbell's insistence on the existence of archetypes that I find most disturbing. Consider this passage from *Myths to Live By:* "All my life, as a student of mythologies, I have been working with these archetypes, and I can tell you they *do* exist and are the same all over the world" (1972, 216; emphasis in original). Jung claimed that there were panhuman, precultural autochthonous images that were supposedly part of a collective, as opposed to a personal unconscious substratum common to all humans, and that these manifestations of the instincts were to be found in dreams and folk narratives. There were only a limited number of these archetypes: the great mother, wise old man, the child, fourness, and so forth. Just as professional folklorists have tended to ignore Campbell and failed to criticize his oeuvre, they have similarly refrained from criticizing Jung and his notion of archetypes. Yet, in sections of bookstores nominally containing books on folklore, we find almost as many Jungian studies of folkloristic subjects as there are books by Campbell. Why has there been no critique by folklorists of the concept of archetype? I believe there is no single idea promulgated by amateurs that has done more harm to serious folklore study than the notion of archetype. I find it invariably cited by ignorant students, as well as equally uninformed members of the general public in the "q and a" period whenever I have occasion to give a public lecture on folklore. The problem with archetype, aside from the unwarranted assumption of psychic unity and universalism, is a practical one of simple identification of such, as is all too clear in the classic essay by Jung on the child archetype. Quoting Jung,

> Often the child is formed after the Christian model. . . . Sometimes the child appears in the cup of a flower, or out of a golden egg, or as the centre of a mandala. In dreams it often appears as a dreamer's son or daughter or as a boy, youth, or young girl, occasionally it seems to be of exotic origin, Indian or Chinese, with a dusky skin, or appearing more cosmically, surrounded by stars or with a starry coronet, or as the king's son or the witch's child with daemonic attributes. Seen as a special instance of "the treasure hard to attain motif" the child motif is extremely variable and assumes all manners of shapes, such as the jewel, the pearl, the flower, the chalice, the golden egg, the quaternary, the

golden ball and so on. It can be interchanged with these and similar images almost without limit.

The critical methodological question is How can one possibly recognize this archetype when it appears in so many guises? How do we know when we come upon a "golden egg" in a folktale that it is a manifestation of the child archetype? Here one must recall Jung's own methodological dictum: archetypes are by definition *unknowable*. One can only approach them asymptotically or tangentially. Jung reiterates this point again and again. So, if archetypes are unknowable, how can we know them? One additional theoretical difficulty is that these supposed archetypes are allegedly panhuman and precultural. Because they are precultural, they are only marginally affected by cultural conditioning. One can easily understand why cultural anthropologists, whose primary working definitional and operational concept is "culture," would not be much interested in a theory that postulated *pre*cultural entities, whether stemming from sociobiology or from Jungian dogma. Incidentally, I blame Freud, in part, for Jung's postulation of the existence of archetypes in a collective unconscious. One of Freud's most grievous errors was his belief that Haeckel's biological discovery that "ontogeny recapitulates phylogeny" applied equally to mental products. In an attempt to explain the multiple existences of certain recurring fantasies—for example, seduction by an adult, observation of parental intercourse, and the threat of castration—he offered the following speculation:

> Whence comes the need for these phantasies and the material for them? There can be no doubt that their sources lie in the instincts; but it has still to be explained why the same phantasies with the same content are created on every occasion. I am prepared with an answer which I know will seem daring to you. I believe that these primal phantasies, as I should like to call them, and no doubt a few others as well are a phylogenetic endowment. In them the individual reaches beyond his own experience into primeval experience at points where his own experience has been too rudimentary. It seems to me quite possible that all the things that are told to us to-day in analysis as phantasy—the seduction of children, the inflaming of sexual excitement by observing parental intercourse, the threat of castration or rather castration itself—were once real occurrences in the primeval times of the human family and that children in their phantasies are simply filling in the gaps in individual truth with prehistoric truth. (1916, 370–71, 1987)

This is an unequivocal, if dubious, statement. If an individual lacks a symbol or fantasy in his or her own life, that symbol or fantasy will be provided through the ontogenetic recapitulation of phylogeny. Probably the most famous, or infamous, example of Freud's application of this principle is the conclusion of *Totem and Taboo* (1946). After acknowledging that the mere thought of killing his father on the part of a son could cause guilt, in the end Freud decided that it was an actual historical act of patricide arising from the primal horde's band brothers uniting to kill their father that accounted for the Oedipus complex and totemism and taboo. This, according to Freud, is because supposedly primitive man, unlike modern man, is not inhibited and accordingly "the thought is directly converted into the deed." The last lines of *Totem and Taboo* are a direct result of Freud's phylogenetic bias: "For that reason I think we may well assume in the case we are discussing, though without vouching for the absolute certainty of the decision, that 'In the beginning was the deed'" (1938, 930).

Freud's phylogenetic inheritance fantasy is clearly comparable to Jung's "collective unconscious." The error in part consists of trying to make psychology into history. Freud's whole theoretical basis for psychoanalysis was essentially the same as nineteenth-century folklore theory, specifically, the doctrine of survivals stemming from unilinear evolutionary theory. Adult neurotic symptoms were in essence survivals from a traumatic situation that had occurred in infancy or early childhood. To understand or explain the apparently irrational symptoms, the analyst had to reconstruct the fuller picture from early childhood by means of free associations and dream content. This is clearly parallel to what Andrew Lang described as "the method of Folklore." Lang, in comparing archaeology and folklore, remarks, "Here is a form of study, Folklore, which collects and compares the similar but immaterial relics of old races, the surviving superstitions and stories, the ideas which are in our time but not of it" ([1884] 2005, 11). The theory was based on the nineteenth-century child-savage equation. As savages passed through barbarism en route to civilization, so children passed through adolescence en route to adulthood. To understand adult folklore (that is, survivals in civilization), one needs to find the fuller form existing among present-day savage (or primitive) societies. In Lang's words, "The method is when an apparently irrational and anomalous custom is found in any country, to look for a country where a similar practice is found, and where the practice is no longer irrational and anomalous, but in harmony with the manners and ideas of the people among whom it prevails. . . . Our method, then, is to compare the seeming meaningless customs and manners of civilized races with the similar customs and manners which exist among the uncivilized and still retain their meaning" (1884, 21). Finally, Lang concludes, "Folklore represents, in the midst of a civilized race, the savage ideas out of which civilisation has been evolved" (25). Freud also saw a parallel between ontogeny and phylogeny. In his foreword to the German edition of Captain John G. Bourke's *Scatalogic Rites of All Nations,* which he wrote at the request of Viennese folklorist Friedrich Krauss, Freud wrote, "The science of folklore has travelled in other paths but nonetheless it has arrived at the same results as psychoanalytic investigations. It shows us how imperfectly various peoples have succeeded in repressing their scatalogic tendencies and how the treatment of the excremental functions on various levels of civilization approaches the infantile stage of human life. It demonstrates to us the perdurance of the primitive, truly ineradicable coprophilic interests . . . in usages connected with popular custom, magical practice, cult acts and the therapeutic art" (1934, ix). This may also illuminate Freud's fascination with archaeology, which also demonstrated the governing intellectual paradigm of the nineteenth century, namely, reconstruction of the past. A shard, like a superstition or a neurotic symptom, was a survival from the past, but a survival that could aid in the reconstruction of that past.

All this is not to excuse Jung's concept of the collective unconscious, but only to show that Freud's thought might have been directly or indirectly one of the sources of this mystical idea. There is yet another theoretical difficulty with the Jungian archetype, and this concerns the unconcealed Christian content of some archetypes. I have already referred to Jung's specific mention of the Christian connection to the child archetype. Much more disturbing, however, is Jung's claim that Jesus Christ is an archetype. In his essay "Aion," Jung asks, "Is the *self* a symbol of Christ, or is Christ a symbol of the *self*?" His answer: "In the present study I have affirmed the latter alternative. I have tried to show how the traditional Christ-image concentrates upon itself the characteristics of an archetype—the archetype of the self" (1958, 36). I am not putting words in Jung's mouth. He adds in an italicized sentence, "Christ exemplifies the archetype of the self," and a footnote invites the reader "Cf. my observations on Christ as archetype in 'A Psychological Approach or the Dogma of the Trinity'" (1958, 36). If we keep in mind that archetypes are assumed to be panhuman, that would constitute a most egregious example of extreme ethnocentrism, not to mention arrogance and hubris or orientalism—namely, to assume that all peoples have a built-in archetypal Christian part of their consciousness regardless of their cultural and racial heritage. Jung states, "The primitive mentality does not invent myths, it experiences them" (1958, 117). Presumably that would also apply to Christian archetypes. Actually, it was precisely Jung's Christian bias that made him so attractive to Freud as a possible successor in order to make psychoanalysis more acceptable to a non-Jewish public, but the extension of that bias into myth as a form of folklore is simply not intellectually defensible or tenable.

The Jungian underpinnings of Campbell's approach to folklore put the approach outside the limits of academic folkloristics. The universalistic premise of psychic unity, coupled with the claim that archetypes are inherited, leaves little room for the influence of cultural relativism and the formation of oicotypes. The inheritance issue is a controversial one. Listen to what Jung himself says about it. In the preface to *Psyche and Symbol*, published in 1958, not long before Jung died in 1961, he said the following:

> Mind is not born as a *tabula rasa*. Like the body it has its pre-established individual definiteness, namely forms of behavior. They become manifest in the ever-recurring patterns of psychic functioning. [Just] as the weaver bird will build its nest infallibly in its accustomed form. [This type of theory invariably makes reference to well-known natural instinctual behavior: birds are not taught how to make nests nor beavers to build dams, thereby arguing by false analogy.] The archetypes are by no means useless archaic survivals or relics. They are living entities which cause the praeformation of numinous ideas or dominant representations. . . . It is important to bear in mind that my concept of the "archetypes" has been frequently misunderstood as a kind of philosophical speculation. [Please pay attention to how Jung clarifies this apparent misunderstanding.] In reality they belong to the realm of the activities of the instincts and in that sense they represent inherited forms of psychic behaviour. (1958, xv–xvi)

It is hard to believe that anyone could accept such a mystical notion as a viable concept in folklore research, but Campbell did. What are we to make of the coffee-table books full of images of alleged archetypes? Of course, it is possible to produce images of mothers from different cultures, but this does not constitute hard evidence of the existence of a Great Mother archetype—only that all cultures have mothers and images of them, but hardly the same image. Even the Christian images of Jesus and the Virgin Mary differ radically within western cultures, typically taking on the physical racial features of the painters of the images or their patrons. If infantile conditioning is critical with respect to man-God relations as Freud argued in *The Future of an Illusion* (1928), then to the extent that infantile conditioning varies from culture to culture, so man-God relations will vary accordingly, and thus there are different myths in different cultures. The constants are not archetypes, but human relationships. There are parent-child relationships in all cultures, and hence there are parent-child struggles in folklore around the world.

When Campbell wrote his 1944 commentary on the Grimm tales for Pantheon, he did his homework. He cited tale types, *The Motif-Index*, and all the scholarly apparatus contained in the writings of folklorists of that time. He even mentioned the historic-geographic method, a.k.a. the Finnish method, as the preferred form of the comparative method employed by folklorists to trace the development and diffusion of a particular folk narrative, but he claimed in a footnote that Franz Boas was a practitioner of the method. During his Columbia years, Campbell actually studied with Boas and, in any case, should have known that Boas never once used the Finnish method. But Campbell's "little bit of knowledge" points to one of our problems. Folklorists have had some success in publicizing the results of our efforts for the past two centuries such that members of other disciplines, after a minimum of reading, believe they are qualified to speak authoritatively about folkloristic matters. It seems that the world is full of self-proclaimed experts in folklore and a few, such as Campbell, have been accepted as such by the general public (and public television, in the case of Campbell). I cannot tell you how many students as well as applicants to the folklore program at Berkeley include in their statements of interest that they have read and enjoyed Campbell's writings. I suppose, in that sense, we owe him a lot for getting people interested in our discipline. The problem is that so many have read only Campbell and know little else about folkloristics.

There are, in my opinion, two other factors that contribute to the low level of folkloristics in the academy: (1) the loss of previous knowledge and (2) intimidation by informants. The loss of previously known facts is perhaps partly attributable to the veritable explosion of knowledge in virtually all fields. It has become increasingly diffi-cult to keep up with all that is written in folkloristics and the myriad journals and monograph series around the world. Bibliographies, computer databases, and search engines help, to some extent, but there are still too many instances of reinventing the wheel. The issue of information retrieval is exacerbated by the growing number of amateurs purporting to represent our field. They are blissfully ignorant of earlier studies of their subject matter. I have already mentioned Campbell's failure to reference either Otto Rank or Lord Raglan's earlier delineations of the hero pattern, and there are count-less other examples.

In the mid-1940s, classicist Rhys Carpenter gave the prestigious Sather Lectures at the University of California, Berkeley, published later as *Folktale, Fiction and Saga in the Homeric Epics* (1946). In a book with that title one would think there might have been at least a mention of AT 1137, The Ogre Blinded (Polyphemos), or the motif in which Odysseus put an oar on his shoulder and walked inland in search of a community that did not know what it was (Hansen 1990; 2002, 371–78). But no such references are to be found. Instead, we find a poorly argued proposition that the *Odyssey* contains the frame-work of the folktale of the bear's son, a hypothesis Carpenter pro-posed after reading the scholarship (by Friedrich Panzer and others) maintaining that Beowulf was derived from that tale type. We have had the Tale Type Index since 1910 and *The Motif-Index* since 1932. Not only could a classicist in 1946 get away with not citing such obvious folktale elements in the *Odyssey*, but, even worse, a major press could publish a book without having obtained competent pre-publication reviews by folktale specialists. One has only to compare the Carpenter book with Bill Hansen's recently published magnifi-cent *Ariadne's Thread: A Guide to International Tales found in Classical Literature* (2002) to see the difference between research by a classicist posing as someone with knowledge of folklore and a classicist who is an authentic full-fledged folklorist.

Let me cite another example of "lost knowledge." In 1955, Ray William Frantz completed a doctoral dissertation at the University of Illinois titled *The Place of Folklore in the Creative Art of Mark Twain,* just one of a considerable number of studies of Twain's interest in and use of folklore in his classic writings. Frantz published some of his findings in his article, "The Role of Folklore in *Huckleberry Finn"* (1956). His work was similar to that of Victor Royce West, who wrote "Folklore in the Works of Mark Twain" in 1930, drawing from his 1928 master's thesis at the University of Nebraska. These and other various attempts (cf. Jones 1984) to demonstrate Twain's definite interest in folklore could have been strongly enhanced by simply examining the membership of the American Folklore Society during its early years. In the very first issue of the *Journal of American Folklore,* we find included on a list of the "Members of the American Folk-Lore Society" one S. L. Clemens of Hartford, Connecticut. Not only was Twain a charter member of the American Folklore Society, but he remained a member for at least five years according to the membership lists in volumes one through five. This means that he received *JAF* for its initial five years of publication, and we may logically assume that he may well have read some of its contents. In any case, given the fact that Frantz and none of the many other critics who have been concerned with Twain's possible interest in folklore have ever mentioned his membership in AFS, we can point to this omission as a prima facie instance of a "loss of knowledge." This kind of factual information like tale types such as 1137, Polyphemus, comprise knowledge available to any true scholar, and part of our task as professional folklorists is to remind our students and our colleagues of the existence of such knowledge. I would also classify as "lost knowledge" Montenyohl's assertion that "folkloristics" is a modern term.

But if "lost knowledge" is an impediment to making advances in folkloristics, so also is what I would call "intimidation by informants." Two folklorists, both major scholars whom I personally admire very much and whose publications constitute hallmarks of the highest-quality scholarship, are both advocates of a policy that insists on not writing anything that might possibly offend any informant. One of these great folklorists insists that his informants are his friends and he wouldn't dream of saying anything in print that they might find insulting or offensive. He expresses his satisfaction in a sentence in perhaps his magnum opus: "One problem down. I had written and lost no friends" (Glassie 1982, 33). I understand that the rapport achieved in successful fieldwork often results in firm, if not lifelong, warm friendships. But giving informants drafts of articles and monographs to vet with the right of veto power or, at the very least, the right to exercise censorship, I find unacceptable. Folkloristics, like any branch of learning, should not devolve into a popularity contest. What if doctors felt it was morally reprehensible to ever tell a patient of a serious disease that required immediate remedial action? This would surely not be in the patient's ultimate best interest. Although there is no need to deliberately offend an informant, there is a need to make the best possible and most enlightening analysis of any data elicited from that informant. If folklorists are afraid of saying anything their informants might not like, the field will never become more than mountains of unanalyzed texts accumulating in folklore archives.

Sometimes the issues involve more serious ethical questions as is the case with our second major folklorist. In this instance, the folklorist collected Navajo folklore for several decades, his expertise so extensive that he was invited to be the sole non-Navajo speaker in a lecture series for a purely Navajo audience. This was surely a great compliment to this folklorist. After lecturing on Coyote stories to this audience, he was startled by a question posed by an elderly singer: "Are you ready to lose a member of your family?" It turned out that there was a level of meaning of the Coyote stories that the folklorist had not been aware of, a level that had to do with witchcraft, and the questioner was trying to warn the folklorist that he was on the edge of potentially dangerous territory with his research. The folklorist took the warning to heart. In an essay written on this incident, he remarked, "Just as a folklorist needs to know where to begin, so one needs to recognize where to stop and I have decided to stop here" (Toelken 1987, 400). He continued, "Rather, as far as discussion of the Coyote tales is concerned, I intend to avoid the information myself, as unscientific and as unscholarly as that may seen. Indeed, in that regard, this is an un-scholarly non-essay, an un-report on what I am not going to be doing with texts recorded over the past twenty-five years" (400). The story is even worse. It is one thing to voluntarily desist from studying one's field data; it is quite another to destroy that data. In this case, the folklorist had a problem once his principal informant died. He knew that the Navajo feel obliged to avoid any interaction with the dead, which includes listening to the recorded voice of someone deceased. In consultation with his deceased informant's widow, the folklorist boxed up sixty-plus hours of original field recording tapes (as well as copies he had used in classes and lectures) and sent them to the widow by registered mail, knowing full well she would be obliged to destroy them. In his essay on the subject in *JAF*, he describes how he came to make this painful decision (1998). My view is that not only has he deprived the academic world of data that may not be able to be replicated, but also that the Navajo themselves have lost a precious resource. We know that many Native Americans have been grateful for earlier work by folklorists and anthropologists in preserving parts of their culture that have unfortunately faded away with the decimation of their populations and their acculturation into mainstream American culture. This is no doubt an extreme example of informant intimidation, but I fear for our field of folkloristics if our very best scholars are timid about analyzing their data or, worse yet, impelled to destroy that data. The field cannot possibly advance if data is destroyed or if we are afraid to analyze it fully for fear of offending someone, either an informant or a colleague.

I have had several personal brushes with would-be intimidation. The first occurred in the late 1960s. I had completed a coauthored study of Turkish verbal dueling. Realizing that some of the data included material that would be considered obscene by most middle-class Americans, I was uncertain where to submit it. I decided to submit it to *South Folklore Quarterly* and I wrote a cover letter to the editor Butler Waugh, who has a doctorate in folklore from Indiana, explaining that I would understand if he could not accept the paper for publication. I was surprised and delighted to hear from him that he liked the paper and accepted it for publication. Six or so months after the paper had been accepted, I received an unexpected letter from Edwin Capers Kirkland. Waugh had moved from the University of Florida to Florida International University in Miami, and Kirkland was the temporary *acting* editor of *SFQ*. The letter informed me that he was very sorry, but it turned out that *SFQ* would not be able or willing to publish my Turkish verbal dueling paper after all. The reason given was not about the cogency of my argument or the accuracy of the reportage of the data, but that the article might offend the regents of the University of Florida. I did not feel this was a legitimate reason for the paper's rejection, especially when the official editor of the journal had previously accepted it. I wrote a strong letter of protest to Kirkland, not asking for reconsideration, but complaining that this was not a valid reason for rejecting the paper. Some of the older members of the American Folklore Society may remember this incident because my revenge consisted of sending a copy of my letter to every major folklorist I knew on the grounds that I wanted to let my colleagues know that an acceptance from *SFQ* might be nullified at a later date. Needless to say, I bitterly resented this gutless and spineless editorial decision, although I was later pleased that the paper in question did appear in *JAF* in 1970.

A second encounter with intimidation or censorship resulted from the last time I had occasion to address this society. It was my presidential address delivered more than twenty years ago at the annual AFS meetings in Pittsburgh in 1980. Because such presidential addresses are routinely published in *JAF*, I sent the final manuscript to the editor for consideration. Because the presentation was quite long, he quite rightly sent it on to the AFS publications editor. Eventually, I received a rejection letter. The reason for the rejection was not because of poor writing, faulty argument, or insufficient data, but rather, that the research was an insult to AFS members of German-American descent. I found this reasoning absurd and insulting, as I am myself an American of partly German descent, but I did realize that the name of the publications editor suggested that she herself was of German-American heritage. Whether the editor actually sent it out for review, I have no way of knowing. The point is that, even if the work was insulting to German-Americans, this is not an intellectually valid reason not to publish a well-researched paper or monograph. As most of you know, the book was published, but not until 1984. The AFS rejection surely contributed to the four-year delay in publication.

I might also mention en passant that I have actually had essays rejected from not one but two different festschrifts on the grounds that the contributions would offend readers in a particular part of the world. For the Ortutay festschrift in Hungary, I submitted my comparison of ethnic jokes about Jews and Polish Americans. Eventually, I was informed by the editors that there was a pact among members of the Eastern bloc not to insult fellow members. Hence, it was against Hungarian law to publish any jokes making fun of Polish people. The editors, however, said that, if I wanted to revise my submission, the jokes about Jews could remain. Considering that the whole point of my essay was to compare the two sets of stereotypes, there was no way I could remove all the Polish jokes. And, of course, I was personally outraged at the suggestion that it was perfectly all right for the anti-Jewish jokes to be published. I might observe that it is not easy or common to be rejected from festschrift volumes, but I have managed it twice. The second occasion involved my essay on East European political jokes being rejected from the Felix Oinas festschrift because prospective readers in the Soviet Union might be offended by it. This was very similar to what happened when I submitted an earlier essay on Romanian jokes to the *East European Quarterly*. The editor of that journal rejected the essay after admitting that he knew most of the jokes and knew they were traditional but feared subscriptions to the journal from Eastern Europe would be cancelled if the essay appeared in the journal. The rejection from the Oinas festschrift made me especially sad because, as a former student of his, I was quite devoted to the late Oinas and I was pretty sure that he personally would have been pleased to have my essay included. As a matter of principle, I decided to decline the invitation to submit a substitute "nonoffensive" essay in its place.

My latest encounter with would-be intimidation occurred in one of my most recent research efforts, in which I applied a folkloristic theory, oral-formulaic to be precise, to the *Qur'an*. I was advised by colleagues both here and abroad not to carry out the study. It was not safe to do so, I was told repeatedly. Upon reading my completed application of oral formulaic theory to the *Qur'an* (Dundes 2003), one trusted colleague eventually confessed that, of course, I was absolutely right in my analysis but it was just not politically correct to have done it. In the Islamic world, applying any theory previously employed in the analysis of secular data to the *Qur'an* would be an enterprise deemed blasphemous, and in the West scholars could in theory have carried out the research but would not dream of doing so for fear of offending their colleagues in the Arab world. As a result, neither the Arab scholars could make this effort nor would the western scholars choose to do so. Censorship is one thing, but self-censorship is in my view a form of academic cowardice. Accordingly, I have spent much of my career resisting attempts at intimidation that might lead to self-censorship. In this instance, it was left for a non-Islamic folklorist to carry out this modest project. In my career, I have never been afraid of offending either informants or colleagues. Whether the group in question consists of football players, Germans, or Orthodox Jews, it makes no difference. My credo remains: Folklore is to be analyzed as best I am able, and the chips will fall where they may. On the day when I become afraid of making an analysis that some may find distasteful or offensive, I shall know that I am on my deathbed.

I hope that this survey of "gloom and doom" is not taken by younger folklorists as discouragement. Yes, the decline of folklore programs is worrisome, the inroads made by amateurs and popularizers are to be condemned, and the loss of knowledge and intimidation by informants is to be decried, but all is not lost. There is as much folklore in the world as ever, and the challenge of collecting and analyzing has never been more exciting. When my wife Carolyn and I visited the Baltics this past summer, I was greatly encouraged to see the tremendous folkloristic energy at Estonia's University of Tartu. I believe Estonia is well on the way to rivaling its neighbor Finland as the prime mover of folklore scholarship in the world today. And Latvia and Lithuania are also major players in contemporary international folkloristic of the twenty-first century. I find the enthusiasm for folklore and the high level of folklore scholarship in these countries very encouraging. In my four-volume set *Concepts: Folklore,* just published (2005), I have not hesitated to draw upon the superior folklore scholarship from the Baltics as well as Finland. Folkloristics is certainly not dead in those areas of the globe.

Richard Dorson ended his classic *American Folklore* with the sentence, "The idea that folklore is dying out is itself a kind of folklore" (1959, 278). Now, I do not actually approve of his use, or misuse, of the word "folklore" in the latter part of that sentence—it indulges in the all too prevalent stereotype meaning of folklore as fallacy or error—but I do think the sentiment may be just as applicable to folkloristics as it continues to be to folklore. Barbara Kirshenblatt-Gimblett, another of our small band of folklore theorists, seems to echo Dorson's sentiment when she says, in another of the many essays concerned with questioning the name of our discipline, "Ours is a discipline predicated on a vanishing subject" (1996, 249). Dan Ben-Amos, another major theorist, is even more pessimistic in his important essay, "Toward a Definition of Folklore in Context," when he asserts, "If the initial assumption of folklore research is based on the disappearance of its subject matter, there is no way to prevent the science from following the same road" (1972, 14), in retrospect a sad prophecy of what has happened at the University of Pennsylvania. But folklore is not vanishing; on the contrary, folklore continues to be alive and well in the modern world, due in part to increased transmission via e-mail and the Internet. And, as I have indicated, the idea that folkloristics as a discipline is dying out is simply not true either. To paraphrase Mark Twain, charter member of the American Folklore Society, "Reports of folkloristics' death have been greatly exaggerated." So as my last hurrah, let me conclude with: hurrah for folklore, hurrah for folkloristics, and hurrah for the American Folklore Society.

References

Aitken, Barbara. 1928. "Day-Dreams in the Spanish Ballads." *Psyche* 9: 44–55.

Ben-Amos, Dan. 1972. "Toward a Definition of Folklore in Context." In *Toward New Perspectives in Folklore*, ed. Américo Paredes and Richard Bauman, pp. 3–15. Austin: University of Texas Press.

———. 1998. "The Name is the Thing." *Journal of American Folklore* 111(441): 257–80.

Bendix, Regina. 1998. "Of Names, Professional Identities, and Disciplinary Futures." *Journal of American Folklore* 111(441): 235–46.

Bourke, John Gregory. 1934. *Scatalogic Rites of All Nations*. New York: American Anthropological Society.

Brewster, Paul G. 1972. *The Incest Theme in Folksong*. FF Communications No. 212. Helsinki: Academia Scientiarum Fennica.

Brunvand, Jan Harold. [1968] 1998. *The Study of American Folklore: An Introduction*. New York: W.W. Norton & Company.

Campbell, Joseph. [1949] 1956. *The Hero with a Thousand Faces*. New York: Meridian Books.

———. 1951. "Bios and Mythos: Prolegomena to a Science of Mythology." In *Psychoanalysis and Culture: Essays in Honor of Géza Róheim*, ed. George B. Wilbur and Warner Muensterberger, pp. 329–43. New York: International Universities Press.

———. 1959. *The Masks of God*. New York: Viking Press.

———. 1960. "Primitive Man as Metaphysician." In *Culture in History*, ed. Stanley Diamond, pp. 380–92. New York: Columbia University Press.

———. 1968. *Creative Mythology*. New York: The Viking Press.

———. 1972. *Myths to Live By*. Foreword by Johnson E. Fairchild. New York: Viking Press.

Campbell, Joseph, and Michael Toms. 1990. *An Open Life*. New York: Harper & Row.

Carpenter, Rhys. 1946. *Folk Tale, Fiction and Saga in the Homeric Epics.* Berkeley: University of California Press.

Doniger, Wendy. 2000. *The Bedtrick: Tales of Sex and Masquerade.* Chicago: University of Chicago Press.

Dorfman, John. 1997. "That's All, Folks!" *Lingua Franca* 7(8): 8–9.

Dorson, Richard M. 1959. *American Folklore.* Chicago: University of Chicago Press.

Dundes, Alan. 1965. *The Study of Folklore.* Englewood Cliffs, N.J.: Prentice-Hall.

——. 1976. "Projection in Folklore: A Plea for Psychoanalytic Semiotics." *Modern Language Notes* 91: 1500–33.

——. 1987. "The Psychoanalytic Study of the Grimms' Tales with Special Reference to 'The Maiden Without Hands' (AT 706)." *Germanic Review* 52: 50–65.

——, ed. 1988. *The Flood Myth.* Berkeley: University of California Press.

——. 2002. "Projective Inversion in the Ancient Egyptian 'Tale of Two Brothers.'" *Journal of American Folklore* 115(457/458): 378–94.

——. 2003. *Fables of the Ancients?: Folklore in the Qur'an.* Lanham: Rowman & Littlefield.

——, ed. 2005. *Folklore: Critical Concepts in Literary and Cultural Studies,* 4 vols. London: Routledge.

Egan, Linda. 1996. "Patriarcado de mi vida, tu castigo estoy sufriendo: El fondo histórico-psíquico del romance-corrido *Delgadina*." *Bulletin of Hispanic Studies* 73: 361–76.

Ellwood, Robert. 1999. *The Politics of Myth: A Study of C. G. Jung, Mircea Eliade and Joseph Campbell.* Albany: State University of New York Press.

Foley, John Miles. 1988. *The Theory of Oral Composition.* Bloomington: Indiana University Press.

Frantz, Ray William, Jr. 1928. *The Future of an Illusion.* London: Hogarth Press.

——. 1934. Foreword. In *Scatalogic Rites of All Nations* by John G. Bourke, pp. vii–ix. New York: American Anthropological Society.

——. 1938. *The Basic Writings of Sigmund Freud.* New York: Modern Library.

——. 1946. *Totem and Taboo: Resemblances between the Psychic Lives of Savages and Neurotics.* Translated by A. A. Brill. New York: Random House.

——. 1955. *The Place of Folklore in the Creative Art of Mark Twain.* PhD diss., University of Illinois.

——. 1956. "The Role of Folklore in *Huckleberry Finn.*" *American Literature* 38: 314–27.

Freud, Sigmund. 1916. *Introductory Lectures on Psycho-Analysis,* Vols. 15 and 16 of *The Standard Edition.* London: Hogarth Press.

——. 1987. *A Phylogenetic Fantasy.* Cambridge: Belknap Press of Harvard University Press.

Georges, Robert A. 1991. "Earning, Appropriating, Concealing, and Denying the Identity of Folklorist." *Western Folklore* 50: 3–12.

Georges, Robert A., and Michael Owen Jones. 1995. *Folkloristics: An Introduction.* Bloomington: Indiana University Press.

Glassie, Henry. 1982. *Passing the Time in Ballymenone.* Philadelphia: University of Pennsylvania Press.

Goldberg, Harriet. 2000. *Motif-Index of Folk Narratives in the Pan-Hispanic Romancero.* Tempe: Arizona Center for Medieval and Renaissance Studies.

Hansen, Gregory. 1997. "The End of Folklore and the Task of Thinking." *Folklore Forum* 28(2): 99–101.

Hansen, William. 1990. "Odysseus and the Oar: A Folkloric Approach." In *Approaches to Greek Myth*, ed. Lowell Edmunds, pp. 241–72. Baltimore: Johns Hopkins University Press.

———. 2002. *Ariadne's Thread: A Guide to International Tales Found in Classical Literature.* Ithaca, N.Y.: Cornell University Press.

Herrera-Sobek, María. 1986. "*La Delgadina:* Incest and Patriarchal Structure in a Spanish/Chicano Romance-Corrido." *Studies in Latin American Popular Culture* 5: 90–107.

Hultkrantz, Åke. 1960. *General Ethnological Concepts.* Copenhagen: Rosenkilde and Bagger.

Jackson, Bruce. 1985. "Folkloristics." *Journal of American Folklore* 98(387): 95–101.

Jones, Steven Swann. 1984. *Folklore and Literature in the United States: An Annotated Bibliography of Studies of Folklore in American Literature.* New York: Garland Publishing.

Jung, C. G. 1958. *Psyche and Symbol: A Selection from the Writings of C. G. Jung,* ed. Violet S. de Laszlo. Garden City: Doubleday Anchor Books.

Kirshenblatt-Gimblett, Barbara. 1985. "Di *folkloristik:* A Good Yiddish Word." *Journal of American Folklore* 98(389): 331–34.

———. 1996. "Topic Drift: Negotiating the Gap between the Field and Our Name." *Journal of Folklore Research* 33: 245–54.

Köhler, Reinhold. 1887. "Folk-lore or Folklore." In *Brockhaus' Conversations-Lexikon, Supplement-band,* pp. 335–336. Leipzig: Brockhaus.

Korff, Gottfried. 1996. "Change of Name as a Change of Paradigm: The Renaming of Folklore Studies Departments at German Universities as an Attempt at 'Denationalization.'" *Europaea* 2(2): 9–32.

Lang, Andrew. [1884] 2005. "The Method of Folklore." In *Folklore: Critical Concepts in Literary and Cultural Studies,* Vol. IV *Folkloristics: Theories and Methods,* ed. Alan Dundes, pp. 39–49. London: Routledge.

Larsen, Stephen, and Robin Larsen. 1993. *A Fire in the Mind: The Life of Joseph Campbell.* New York: Anchor Books.

Lefkowitz, Mary R. 1990. "The Myth of Joseph Campbell." *American Scholar* 59: 429–34.

Leland, Charles G. 1890–1892. "Aus dem Begrüssungschreiben an die Gesellschaft." *Ethnologische Mitteilungen aus Ungarn* 2(1): 2–3.

Locke, Liz. 1998. "Is Folklore Finished?" *Lingua Franca* 7(10): 68.

Mariscal Hay, Beatriz. 2002. "Incest and the Traditional Ballad." *Acta Ethnographica* 47: 19–27.

Montenyohl, Eric. 1996. "Divergent Paths: On the Evolution of 'Folklore' and 'Folkloristics.'" *Journal of Folklore Research* 33: 232–35.

Nikhilananda, Swami. 1936. "Sri Ramakrishna and Spiritual Renaissance." In *The Cultural Heritage of India, Sri Ramakrishna Centenary Memorial* vol. 2, pp. 441–617. Calcutta: Belur Math.

Oring, Elliott. 1991. "On the Future of American Folklore Studies: A Response." *Western Folklore* 50: 75–81.

———. 1998. "Anti Anti-'Folklore.'" *Journal of American Folklore* 111(441): 328–38.

Propp, V. 1968. *Morphology of the Folktale.* Translated by Laurence Scott, intro. Alan Dundes. Austin: University of Texas Press.

Segal, Robert. 1990. "Introduction: In Quest of the Hero." In *In Quest of the Hero* by Otto Rank, Lord Raglan, and Alan Dundes, pp. vii-xli. Princeton, N.J.: Princeton University Press.

Sokolov, Yuriy. [1938] 1971. *Russian Folklore.* Detroit: Folklore Associates.

Toelken, Barre. 1987. "Life and Death in the Navajo Coyote Tales." In *Recovering the Word: Essays on Native American Literature,* ed. Brian Swann and Arnold Krupat, pp. 388–401. Berkeley: University of California Press.

———. 1998. "The Yellowman Tapes, 1966–1997." *Journal of American Folklore* 111(442): 381–91.

West, Victor Royce. 1930. "Folklore in the Works of Mark Twain." *University of Nebraska Studies in Language, Literature, and Criticism* 10: 1–87.

ALAN DUNDES was Professor of Folklore and Anthropology at the University of California, Berkeley. He published more than 250 articles and edited and coedited numerous works, including *The Study of Folklore* (1965) and *International Folkloristics: Classic Contributions by the Founders of Folklore* (1999). His works include *Two Tales of Crow and Sparrow: A Freudian Folkloristic Essay on Caste and Untouchability* (1997), *Folklore Matters* (1989), *From Game to War and Other Psychoanalytic Essays on Folklore* (1997), *Holy Writ as Oral Lit: The Bible as Folklore* (1999), *The Shabbat Elevator and Other Sabbath Subterfuges: An Unorthodox Essay on Circumventing Custom and Jewish Character* (2002), *Fables of the Ancients?: Folklore in the Qur'an* (2003), *Folklore: Critical Concepts in Literary and Cultural Studies* (2005), and several casebooks on the vampire, the walled-up wife, Cinderella, and Oedipus. This address appeared posthumously in the *Journal of American Folklore,* as Dundes died while it was still in press.

Responses

2 America's Antitheoretical Folkloristics

BEGETTING THIS COLLECTION of essays was an American Folklore Society forum in October 2005, which asked the question, "Why is there no 'Grand Theory' in folkloristics?" The origin of the phrase in sociology is explained in the essay by Gary Alan Fine. Talcott Parsons (1902–1979) inscribed "grand theory," which he said "put the analysis of social phenomena on a new track in the broadest possible terms." Not all sociologists, he knew, would accept those broad terms; some still adhered to the empirical level, as folklorists continue to do today (1937, viii–ix). In the AFS forum, the diverse answers arrived at substantial agreement: American folklorists have produced little "grand theory." One speaker even found all the theory folklorists need in the history of philosophy. The two women (Noyes and Mills) spoke in defense of theory that is local, "apt," suited to the audience, and "humble"; the men (Bauman and Fine) reached for something Parsons might have recognized. The essays in this collection, developed from the forum presentations, defend diverse positions, but they largely accept the longstanding concentration in American folkloristics on the quotidian and local. To fill out the picture, John W. Roberts has contributed an unblunted look at the history of American folkloristics, a fuller paper than the brief pieces I solicited from the forum participants. It was originally addressed to a conference in May 2006 at Ohio State University on "Negotiating the Boundaries of Folklore Theory and Practice." For contrast, one other country provides a comparison to the American emphasis: James Dow, America's leading interpreter and translator of folklore studies in Germany, contributes an essay to show the decline in the status of folklore there and the fragmentation of *Volkskunde* studies.

Concentrating on the United States, it is important to be true to the history of the field. Dorothy Noyes and John Roberts point to what American folklorists learned from Franz Boas and William Wells Newell, whose evolutionary assumption is dead today, though folklorists have neither considered nor rejected evolution's newer refinements (Eccles 1989; Falk 2004). No longer are cultural productions seen as monuments to be studied in an archaeological spirit, although many of the folk regard them so. True to their historical moment, folklorists have turned away from the past. "Vernacular practices," writes Roger D. Abrahams on this topic, "are our focus and our hope, not just the waifs and strays or the scattered remains of past societies" (2005, 148). But our historical position, says Dorothy Noyes, is that of the "provincial intellectual," probing "the intimate other of modernity." Characteristic of pragmatic, "can-do" America, our folkloristics is tirelessly inventive of method, without caring to ask what theory the methods are based on. In contrast to literary study, folkloristics has manifested neither a strong interest in theory nor a receptivity to foreign influences (de Man 1986, 5). Also staying close to the history of the field, Richard Bauman christens the common intellectual program the "philology of the vernacular." As Roland Barthes led critics "from work to text," Bauman, Dell Hymes, Erving Goffman, and M. M. Bakhtin have led folklorists from words to the social situation that elicits them. The broad redefinition of "text" in Bauman's previous work to mean the whole of a communicative event in its actual occurrence has amounted to a call to weave theory and formal criticism into ethnography (Hutcheon 1988, 94–101). Bauman calls his philology of the vernacular a prevailing theory, though not the only one. It doesn't prevail in all of the studies that properly belong to folklore. Take mythology, that most alienated branch of folklore study, which has the same philological ancestry and the same history of struggle between the literary and the anthropological. Mythological studies are thematic, moralistic, or historical, but seldom oriented to the vernacular.

Nor, as Bauman notes, is philology the only line of descent for American folklorists of today. Studies of folklife and material culture, also named folklore, trace their descent from William Morris, John Ruskin, anthropologists like Robert Plant Armstrong (Glassie 1999; Vlach 1993; Armstrong 1971), and historians like Lawrence W. Levine (Levine 1977; Joyner 1984). Another line leads to "public folklore"— the presentation of traditional arts to new audiences—which has grown out of festival production, museology, and involvement with broadcast media (Baron and Spitzer 1992). Then there is folk music, which finds its line of descent not only in Johann Gottfried von Herder and Francis James Child, but also in musicology (Evans 1982; Palmer 1981). If mythology, material culture, arts administration, and folk music are all taught in American university departments (surely departments are as local as can be), can any Grand Theory connect them? The absence of a self-conscious theoretical tradition, says Gary Alan Fine, makes it hard for folklorists to build models that transcend the local. Or is that desire what John W. Roberts calls "a frenzied attempt to claim scientific rigor"?

What theory authorizes American folklorists to focus on vernacular practices? What principles do we unwittingly follow in documenting and commenting on folklore? What principles underlie the rules of folkloristic competence (Gardner 1987, 189)? What about a non-Grand Theory? Margaret Mills advocates evaluating theory and interpretation through the eyes of members of the group being studied. How well will they appreciate the interpretation? Might her "low" theory be just the transcending model Gary Alan Fine calls for? Properly theorized, it would reach high (Abrahams 2005). Interpretation by performers and audiences, called "oral literary criticism" (Narayan 1995), touches the same topics as literary theorists do. To pose these questions leads inevitably back to defining the object of our investigation, as John Roberts asserts, and as Michel de Certeau says about history (Revel and Hunt 1995, 441). The definition game, which never ends among us (Ben-Amos 1971; Dundes 1966; Georges and Jones 1995, 231–32), sprang up during the discussion of these papers, as spontaneously as touch football. Discussants were reminded that folklore studies are racked by uncertainties and conflicts, as are many other disciplines (Richter 1994).

There is no Grand Theory in American folkloristics, I believe, because we are uncomfortable with the rhetoric of Grand Theory, because we refuse its authoritarian stance, and because we have gravitated towards the lower strata of societies. In rhetoric, Parsons's Grand Theory style was consistently abstract. His critic C. Wright Mills (1916–1962), no less a Weberian than Parsons, once ridiculed the style by reducing four and five of Parsons's paragraphs to one each of his own, in the reductive spirit of postwar polemics against gobbledygook (Flesch 1946 and 1949). As Gary Alan Fine points out, folklorists could be comfortable with Mills's urging toward "historical and structural contexts" necessary "to describe and explain human conduct and society plainly" (1970, 42). Already in Mills's time, Herbert Halpert was recommending that folklorists "offer us information in context about the area and the informants" (1958, 99). Melville Jacobs, another contemporary, was faulting folklorists for ignoring their own intellectual context, for failing "to learn from the advances in method and theory which were occurring in related fields of inquiry" (1959, 196). Mills could have known from his master Veblen that it's perfectly possible to write abstractly about power relations. Folklorists today could know that from Homi Bhabha, Gayatri Spivak, and (the grandest exemplar) Michel Foucault, if they read them.

But American folklorists practice a different rhetoric, a continual movement between theory and method, which for us is the essence of thoughtful investigation, and which leads towards Dorothy Noyes's "humble" theory. Folklorists agree with certain literary critics: if theory is "an attempt to guide practice from a position above or outside it [and] an attempt to reform practice" by means of a general rationality (Fish 1989, 319; Knapp and Michaels 1985), the effort is futile and misdirected. The present generation of American folklorists takes instead the example of Dell Hymes, who (in Dorothy Noyes's phrase) stays close to the ground, while also always formulating "a theory of the special case" (Hymes 1971, 51). Out of the special cases he treats, Hymes repeatedly sets forth extensive programs, but his generalizations promote ethnographic method, not sustained theory. His most theoretical statement advocates method: "to start from community definitions of situation, activity, purpose, genre, and to discover validly the ways in which communicative means are organized in terms of them" (1975, 350).

The anti-authoritarian stance of American folklorists today is one moment in the sequence of modes of thinking about the folk and their lore. Folkloristic production happens in history, where "the existence of a determinate [set of behaviors classified together] always reflects a certain possibility of experience in the moment of social development in question" (Jameson 1988, 9). At the beginning, eight years before Thoms wrote his note to the *Athenaeum* coining the word *folklore*, the Chartist movement had arisen as a working-class protest against industrialism; Thomas Carlyle soon roared his anti-industrialist response, *Chartism* (1840). William Cobbett was already pleading on behalf of the poor. Thoms's neologism moved to contain the populace ideologically, by ascribing their customs and manners to "the olden time." Just then the studies that came to be known as "English" were arising out of a desire to depoliticize the working class by imparting middle-class ideology in terms of universal values (Eagleton 1983, 25). Thoms's "Folk-lore" was the "counter-distinction to the developing and enveloping capitalist modernity" around him (Limón 1998). Coloring the folk and their lore as politically irrelevant, Thoms's voice was no solitary one, but it is the one prophetic voice that folklorists hark back to. In Thoms's England, as in John Roberts's United States, the spirit of nationalism advanced conceptions of folklore. In the 1970s, when Hymes, Goffman, and William Labov began turning folklore in the direction of descriptive ethnography, a new nationalism and xenophobia pervaded the nation and *On the Road* sounded its paean of praise to the vernacular. There was no "unified theory of expressive behavior" then; there was no "comprehensive, current work on folklore theory" (Burns 1977, 133). There was, however, a movement to democratize the notion of creativity, to recognize that even the powerless carried out aesthetic production as their expression of power. So Hymes defined folkloristics as "the study of communicative behavior with an esthetic, expressive, or stylistic dimension" (1974, 133).

From that definition came the attention to performance (Bauman 1977), but also a fatal political role and a fatal theoretical flaw. Politically, folklore has a role to play in maintaining the power structures existing in American society. Theoretically, if performance can be distinguished from non-performance when one person takes on responsibility before a knowing audience, then "folklore" has been not marked off; it has been dissolved. If *all* speech is to be approached as having an esthetic, expressive, or stylistic dimension (Hymes 1972, 50), then there is no substance to "folklore"; there is instead merely a dimension to be discerned. Isn't that discernment the very making of folkloristics? Isn't that how vernacular architecture, costume, the weaving of rugs, and pottery attain the status of folklore (Glassie 1999)? Any attempt now to frame, out of the practices and methods of American folklorists, a Grand Theory of folklore meets this obstacle: the entity has dissolved. The expression called folkloric ought to be definable by relation to other kinds of production, in order to give ourselves an object of knowledge (Ducrot and Todorov 1972, 107). But it has become impossible to separate folklore from other human activities, except as a product of one moment in that sequence of modes of thinking. "Folklore" is a historically-bounded term with a beginning and (now) an end. It has already been relinquished in some American universities; why not turn "folklore" over to traditional artists and their presenter-producers, who are developing "methods to interpret their traditions before audiences outside of customary performance contexts" (Baron 1999, 195)?

This view arises not through despair at defining the field or getting it more recognition in universities, but rather through trying to discover the nature of creativity. There are two kinds: "the use of an old sentence in a new setting . . . the use of a new sentence in an old setting" (Hymes 1972, 49). If folklorists today want to learn from advances in method and theory in related fields of inquiry (following Melville Jacobs's advice), they could turn for instance to a field like cognitive science. Cognitive linguists propose that all human thinking is metaphorical at base. Metaphor as we see it in a proverb, being a product of human invention, is an elaboration out of universal mental equipment carried by everyone (Lakoff and Turner 1989, 174–79). Cognitive linguists propose to offer convincing, cross- cultural, experimental evidence for the fundamentally metaphorical nature of thought (Lakoff and Johnson 1999). If they convince folklorists of this conception of "human nature," then what requires study in culture comprises a great deal more human behavior than the mere artistic communication of small groups (Ben-Amos 1971, 13). The separation of "folklore" from anthropology, literature, music, and art comes to an end, to be reconstructed on a new basis of knowledge of cognition. Or folklorists may simply continue to ignore the contributions psychology might make to their field, as they have rejected psychoanalytic interpretation.

Acknowledgments

I am grateful to the contributors and to the editors of the *Journal of Folklore Research* for their efforts in assembling these articles.

References

Abrahams, Roger D. 2005. *Everyday Life: A Poetics of Vernacular Practices.* Philadelphia: University of Pennsylvania Press.

Armstrong, Robert Plant. 1971. *The Affecting Presence: An Essay in Humanistic Anthropology.* Urbana: University of Illinois Press.

Baron, Robert. 1999. "Theorizing Public Folklore Practice: Documentation, Genres of Representation, and Everyday Competencies." *Journal of Folklore Research* 36 (2–3): 185–201.

Baron, Robert, and Nicholas R. Spitzer. 1992. *Public Folklore.* Washington: Smithsonian Institution.

Bauman, Richard. 1977. *Verbal Art as Performance.* Prospect Heights, Ill.: Waveland Press.

Ben-Amos, Dan. 1971. "Toward a Definition of Folklore in Context." *Journal of American Folklore* 84 (331): 3–15.

Burns, Thomas A. 1977. "Folkloristics: A Conception of Theory." *Western Folklore* 36 (2): 109–34.

Carlyle, Thomas. 1840. *Chartism.* London: James Fraser.

Ducrot, Oswald, and Tzvetan Todorov. 1972. *Dictionnaire encyclopédique des sciences du langage.* Paris: Éditions du Seuil.

Dundes, Alan. 1966. "The American Concept of Folklore." *Journal of the Folklore Institute* 3: 226–49.

Eagleton, Terry. 1983. *Literary Theory: An Introduction.* Minneapolis: University of Minnesota Press.

Eccles, John C. 1989. *Evolution of the Brain, Creation of the Self.* New York: Routledge.

Evans, David. 1982. *Big Road Blues: Tradition and Creativity in the Folk Blues.* Berkeley: University of California Press.

Falk, Dean. 2004. *Braindance: New Discoveries About Human Origins and Brain Evolution.* Gainesville: University Press of Florida.

Fish, Stanley. 1989. *Doing What Comes Naturally: Change, Rhetoric, and the Practice of Theory in Literary and Legal Studies.* Durham, N. C.: Duke University Press.

Flesch, Rudolf. 1946. *The Art of Plain Talk.* New York: Harper & Row.

———. 1949. *The Art of Readable Writing.* New York: Harper.

Gardner, Howard. 1987. *The Mind's New Science: A History of the Cognitive Revolution.* New York: Basic Books.

Georges, Robert A., and Michael Owen Jones. 1995. *Folkloristics: An Introduction.* Bloomington: Indiana University Press.

Glassie, Henry. 1999. *Material Culture.* Bloomington: Indiana University Press.

Halpert, Herbert. 1958. "Folklore: Breadth Versus Depth." *Journal of American Folklore* 71 (280): 97–103.

Hutcheon, Linda. 1988. *A Poetics of Postmodernism: History, Theory, Fiction.* London: Routledge.

Hymes, Dell. 1971. "The 'Wife' Who 'Goes Out' Like a Man: Reinterpretation of a Clackamas Chinook Myth." In *Structural Analysis of Oral Tradition,* ed. Pierre Maranda and Elli Köngäs Maranda., 49–80. Philadelphia: University of Pennsylvania Press.

———. 1972. "The Contribution of Folklore to Sociolinguistic Research." In *Toward New Perspectives in Folklore,* ed. Américo Paredes and Richard Bauman., 42–50. Austin: University of Texas Press.

————. 1974. *Foundations in Sociolinguistics: An Ethnographic Perspective.* Philadelphia: University of Pennsylvania Press.

————. 1975. "Folklore's Nature and the Sun's Myth." *Journal of American Folklore* 88 (350): 346–69.

Jacobs, Melville. 1959. "Morphology of the Folktale, by Vladimir Propp." *Journal of American Folklore* 72 (284): 195–96.

Jameson, Fredric. 1988. *The Ideologies of Theory: Essays 1971–1986,* vol. 1, Situations of Theory. Minneapolis: University of Minnesota Press.

Joyner, Charles. 1984. *Down by the Riverside: A South Carolina Slave Community.* Urbana: University of Illinois Press.

Kerouac, Jack. 1957. *On the Road.* New York: Viking Press.

Knapp, Steven, and Walter Benn Michaels. 1985. "Against Theory." In *Against Theory: Literary Studies and the New Pragmatism,* ed. W. J. T. Mitchell, 1–30. Chicago: University of Chicago Press.

Lakoff, George, and Mark Johnson. 1999. *Philosophy in the Flesh: The Embodied Mind and Its Challenge to Western Thought.* New York: Basic Books.

Lakoff, George, and Mark Turner. 1989. *More Than Cool Reason: A Field Guide to Poetic Metaphor.* Chicago: University of Chicago Press.

Levine, Lawrence W. 1977. *Black Culture and Black Consciousness: Afro-American Folk Thought from Slavery to Freedom.* Oxford: Oxford University Press.

Limón, José E. 1998. "Folklore—If It Is—Is a Marxist Practice." *Paper presented at the American Folklore Society conference in Portland,* Oregon.

de Man, Paul. 1986. *The Resistance to Theory.* Minneapolis: University of Minnesota Press.

Mills, C. Wright. 1970. [1959] *The Sociological Imagination.* Harmondsworth: Penguin Books.

Narayan, Kirin. 1995. "The Practice of Oral Literary Criticism: Women's Songs in Kangra, India." *Journal of American Folklore* 108 (429): 243–64.

Palmer, Robert. 1981. *Deep Blues.* New York: The Viking Press.

Parsons, Talcott. 1937. *The Structure of Social Action.* New York: Free Press.

Revel, Jacques, and Lynn Hunt, eds. 1995. *Histories: French Constructions of the Past,* trans. Arthur Goldhammer, et al. New York: The New Press.

Richter, David H. 1994. *Falling Into Theory: Conflicting Views on Reading Literature.* Boston: St Martin's Press.

Vlach, John Michael. 1993. *Back of the Big House: The Architecture of Plantation Slavery.* Chapel Hill: University of North Carolina Press.

LEE HARING is Professor Emeritus of English at Brooklyn College of the City University of New York. He has carried out folklore research in Kenya, Madagascar, Mauritius, and the other islands of the Southwest Indian Ocean. He is the author of *Stars and Keys* (IUP, 2007), a collection of folktale translations from the Indian Ocean islands; *Verbal Arts in Madagascar;* the online book *How to Read a Folktale* (http://www .openbookpublishers.com/product/109/), which translates a heroic epic from Madagascar; and numerous scholarly articles.

3 The Sweep of Knowledge: The Politics of Grand and Local Theory in Folkloristics

FOLKLORISTS HAVE ALWAYS been of several minds about the centrality of theory. From the earliest incarnation of folkloristics as "popular antiquities," its mandate (and that of its practioners) has been to gather texts and traditions before they disappear, capturing these endangered creatures, recording, filming, and transcribing them for posterity, as a record of a cultural past. The descriptive goals of our discipline are of inestimable value for preserving the cultural patrimony of humanity.

However, folklorists have rarely been without theory. Their compelling collections of texts lead to the question of what they all mean. Whether scholars have suggested that myths represent astronomical features in symbolic form, that folktales originate from a single source, diffusing through trade routes, or that folk beliefs are corrupted forms of religious faith, they have long attempted to find regularity in the origins, functions, and spread of tradition.

What folklorists have not done as often is to construct perspectives that transcend particular genres, cultures, or settings. This approach to systematizing knowledge has come to be known as "grand theory." As a result, scholars such as the late Alan Dundes have argued vigorously that folkloristics must self-consciously incorporate large-scale, overarching theories of self, society, or narrative, such as those propounded by Freud, Lévi-Strauss, Marx, Propp, or Bakhtin. Dundes tried to move folklore away from its allergy to theory and its preoccupation with the presentation of texts and description of action, remarking on "the continued lack of innovation in what we might term 'grand theory'" (Dundes 2005, 387; Oring 1991).

With regard to theory, academic disciplines are reminiscent of drug markets: we find users, dealers, growers, and even a few abstainers. (There are cops as well, but that is for another discussion on the control function of journal reviews.) Alan Dundes, for example, was primarily a dealer, reminding his colleagues of the utility of the grand theories of others, notably those of Propp and Freud, but not creating a distinctive Dundesian model, an approach that reconceptualizes the arguments of others into a theory-methods package.

For some, the relative absence of disciplinary theory represents a central intellectual dilemma of the discipline, for others it presents a crucial institutional problem. In order to be considered legitimate, must a discipline have its own theory—in its own mind and that of others? Or is a body of users sufficient?

The place of theory in a discipline is a crucial political matter. Theory provides a means of networking scholars in a common project and justifying a discipline. Furthermore, it represents a collective point of reference. Even if some (or many) object to the theoretical formulation (consider rational choice theory in political science, neo-classical theory in economics, or deconstruction in literary theory), there is a center that can be embraced or rejected.

In most disciplines, a division exists between theorists, however defined, and others. Not everyone will describe himself or herself as a theorist (or be so described by others), but some will, and there will be the recognition of a boundary, perhaps hazy, between the groups. Whether armchair or empirical, theorists see themselves as having a different mandate than non-theorists.

Yet, in most disciplines the boundary between theorists and others is hazy and uncertain, and, as a result, a vigorous "What is Theory?" debate often rages. In 2005, Gabriel Abend, a young sociological theorist, argued that in his discipline—the grand home of Grand Theory—theory can be used rhetorically in at least six distinct ways. These approaches include four that are pertinent to folklorists: a) the exegesis of classic texts (such as Von Sydow, Roheim, Propp, or Marx), b) the development of logically interconnected propositions, c) the linkage of concepts to each other, and d) the creation of overarching models—the attempt to construct a grand theory. This is quite a range of scholarly activities, and it leads to debate among those who describe themselves as theorists. It is Abend's contention that when theory serves as a badge of honor such a jumble of images of theory generates confusion. When audiences hear someone speak of needing more theory, they may have several pictures in mind.

Abend suggests that consensus in the meaning of theory is necessary. The order that he proposes must result from that socio-political process by which common knowledge is generated in any epistemic community. It is Abend's hope, perhaps Panglossian, that a scholarly discipline can create a set of shared understandings. This hope is certainly applicable to folklore where the discussions of theory are at a more primitive level than in other social sciences and where theory is often limited to the borrowing of classic texts, but rarely to the construction of Grand Theory.

The term Grand Theory itself has an interesting provenance, a folk politics. The term refers to the attempt by mid-century sociologists to create an interlocked set of concepts to explain social order. We might term such a set of concepts a *Weltanschauung* or a perspective or lens through which a theorist can ascribe meaning to the world. As such it is metaphorically akin to unified field theory in physics, borrowing both the global ambition and perhaps the impossibility of that effort. Grand Theory most typically refers to the work of Talcott Parsons and his *General Theory of Action*, although Marxism might also fall within its purview. At a moment in the 1930s when sociologists endeavored to gain a standing for their field of study in elite American universities (notably at Harvard) by demonstrating that it could provide the social scientific equivalent of physics, Parsons presented a model to understand the functioning of advanced societies. The term Grand Theory, however, was not coined by Parsons, but instead was first used by C. Wright Mills (1959), who intended it as a pejorative and used it to critique Parsons's writings, which Mills saw as being insufficiently focused on how empirical examples bolstered or critiqued over-arching assertions. Mills saw Parsons's analyses as armchair claims-making that did not rely on the detailed examination of cases and that took for granted the desirability of the political status quo. Mills pushed for a theory of localism, an approach that is well suited to the analysis of traditions and folk genres. Mills's warning was prescient; it is advice that folklorists should take to heart: never exclude the empirical and the local.

It was not that Mills was atheoretical, but rather that he questioned the attempt to systematize all social institutions through a single set of concepts that bulldozed the specifics of the case. Mills, and other mid-century sociologists such as Herbert Blumer, felt that an alternate approach to theory held more promise, namely, that of the organizing perspective. Here, a set of concepts helps to provide a lens to make sense of the world. The goal of these concepts was to understand action within the contexts in which they emerged: they were fundamentally local and interactional.

As an example, the idea of performance within folklore serves as an organizing perspective and a particularly influential one. Performance suggests that tradition is known through the fact that it is enacted in particular settings, under the constraint of organizations and institutions, and that performers and audiences are situated within a world of power and meaning that is continually shaped by virtue of performance. Performance theory is also notable in that it reminds us that a theory can systematically explain local phenomena without being primarily descriptive. It has the further disciplinary virtue of having emerged largely from folklore studies itself (e.g., Ben-Amos and Goldstein 1975; Paredes and Bauman 1972), but is now spread throughout the social sciences and humanities. It can be claimed by folklore as a disciplinary creation. Such an organizing perspective has neither the majestic design nor the attempted comprehensiveness of grand theory, but it provides a distinctive way of looking while also taking into account the systematic ways in which local conditions give birth to and support traditions. One might suggest—as some have about the intellectual modesty of performance theory—that systematization is necessary and therefore attempt to push this perspective to the creation of a more formal theory. Such a lens serves better than an unprovable Grand Theory that reveals traces of intellectual hubris and is impossible to evaluate using empirical cases.

Theories and Community

One of the effects of successful theories is to create a network—a folk community. Naming a project leads individuals to recognize that they are working together on a common intellectual project. In addition, it permits scholars to conclude that they belong together. The label helps to create what Diana Crane has famously termed an invisible college, a network of academics who are exploring the same issues (1972).

When I proposed the "Third Force" critique in 1988, I was attempting to create a community that recognized a common task. I used the "Third Force in Folkloristics" to refer to the understanding that folklore genres were not simply developed by individuals and communities, but were shaped by institutions and social structures as well. Folklore developed out of organizational politics and the demands of mercantile relations and state systems. Diffusion, for instance, did not simply happen, but was the consequence of the way that communication channels and trade routes were organized. In my critique I wanted to encourage folklorists who in my view were engaging in a set of implicitly linked projects that took social structure seriously. These scholars were borrowing ideas from various corners of the social sciences, particularly from sociology. Bringing these projects together under a common rubric created a basis for discussion. By connecting the work of scholars such as Linda Dégh, Simon Bronner, Stanley Brandes, Janet Langlois, Joel Best, and Jacqueline Simpson, I tried to outline a common orientation. Although others might easily be added to this list of folklorists who approach texts in relation to social, political, and economic structures, it was intended to suggest that examination of performance without a macrostructural context is fundamentally deficient. This suggestion should return folklorists' attention to one of Alan Dundes's early and classic articles, "Texture, Text, and Context" (Dundes 1964; Fine 1988).

My argument recognizes something important about theory, something that is particularly important for folklorists: theory creates community. This is equally true whether we are talking about Marxism, rational choice theory, neo-functionalism, performance theory, deconstructionism, or feminist standpoint theory. It is not necessary that the writings be entirely consistent; what matters more is that individuals come to believe that they are sharing a common goal. By placing individuals in a social category, recognized by both insiders and outsiders, scholars come to feel that they are linked, creating dialogue as well as establishing boundaries. Theorists, too, can be the folk. There is thus a socio-politics of theoretical clusters in which each cluster has its own social structure (Collins 2000).

But theory is important in another way as well, a way that also pays heed to the politics of a discipline. Just as theory brings people together, most forms of theory bring concepts together. Theory prevents intellectual domains from becoming isolated and creates a network of research projects. Theory knits together empirical projects. The theorist's job is to build bridges, allowing colleagues to recognize the commonalities between projects and preventing folklore from becoming an archipelago of islands of knowledge. This network is important intellectually, but it is also important in giving cohesion and coherence to a discipline, a sense of purpose that sometimes seems perilously absent in folkloristics.

The Politics of Description

At the time of America's bicentennial, folklorists found a new home—a workplace—in federal, state, and municipal governments. This created an applied market with ups and downs for public folklorists, a market in which theory received few rewards. While this provided our discipline institutional standing outside of the academy, these positions often pushed folklorists to emphasize the descriptive, the particular, the unique, the amazing, and the isolated. Governmental agencies gave credit for those projects that spoke to public constituencies, which described rather than analyzed. The institutional demands of these new positions diminished the intellectual power of folklore, and perhaps, as some have argued, contributed to the precarious status of folkloristics within the academy.

Theory is, after all, a status marker among academics, a means by which those outside a discipline come to believe that important matters are being addressed by their colleagues. Theory is not merely descriptive knowledge, but makes the case that it is relevant for other domains. The absence of a strong, self-conscious, and recognized theoretical tradition harms folklore in the academy in a double sense. First, it makes folklore seem of minor relevance to other scholars, and, coupled with a paucity of individuals dedicated to building programs within academic institutions, it leaves folklore vulnerable. Second, however, the absence of a self-conscious theoretical tradition means that folklorists often do not do enough to interact with each other, and do not share and create ideas that transcend a particular project. Theory is a means of generalizing knowledge, of breaking outside of one's empirical circle. Without core concepts—whether these be grand theory or organizing perspectives—folklorists find it hard to build models that transcend the particular and demonstrate that an understanding of folklore helps us to understand all places at all times. This lacuna undermines our confidence as masons of knowledge. Folklorists do not need Grand Theory per se as much as we need ongoing attempts at analytical synthesis that explain the intersection of the local, the collective, and the structural through the power of tradition. As a result, our responsibility is to rise to the challenge of explaining that folklore helps explain Society—and not only societies in all their wondrous uniqueness.

References

Abend, Gabriel. 2005. "The Meaning of Theory." *Paper presented at the American Sociological Association conference*, in Philadelphia.

Ben-Amos, Dan, and Kenneth S. Goldstein, eds. 1975. *Folklore: Performance and Communication*. The Hague: Mouton.

Blumer, Herbert. 1969. *Symbolic Interaction*. Englewood Cliffs: Prentice Hall.

Collins, Randall. 2000. *The Sociology of Philosophies: A Global Theory of Intellectual Change*. Cambridge, Mass.: Harvard University Press.

Crane, Diana. 1972. *Invisible Colleges: Diffusion of Knowledge in Scientific Communities*. Chicago: University of Chicago Press.

Dundes, Alan. 1964. "Texture, Text and Context." *Southern Folklore Quarterly* 28: 251–65.

———. 2005. "Folkloristics in the Twenty-First Century (AFS Invited Presidential Plenary Address, 2004)." *Journal of American Folklore* 118 (470): 385–408.

Fine, Gary Alan. 1988. "The Third Force in American Folklore: Folk Narratives and Social Structure." *Fabula* 29: 342–53.

Mills, C. Wright. 1959. *The Sociological Imagination*. New York: Oxford University Press.

Oring, Elliott. 1991. "On the Future of American Folklore Studies: A Response." *Western Folklore* 50 (1): 75–81.

Paredes, Américo, and Richard Bauman, eds. 1972. *Toward New Perspectives in Folklore*. Austin: University of Texas Press.

Parsons, Talcott and Edward A. Shils, eds. 1951. *Towards a General Theory of Action*. Cambridge Mass: Harvard University Press.

GARY ALAN Fine is John Evans Professor of Sociology at Northwestern University. He received his PhD in social psychology with a minor in folklore and mythology from Harvard University. He is the author (with Patricia Turner) of *Whispers on the Color Line: Rumor and Race in America* and the author of *Manufacturing Tales: Sex and Money in Contemporary Legends*. Most recently he has authored (with Bill Ellis) *The Global Grapevine: Why Rumors of Terrorism, Immigration, and Trade Matter*.

4 What('s) Theory?

THE OBSERVATIONS BELOW remain collage-like, a short suggestion list for a few theoretical endeavors not uniquely ours but profitably pursued by us and shared interdisciplinarily, given the broad domains of expressive life that we prefer to think about.

The base question may be "Am I doing theory (yet)?" Metatheory seems easier to identify, easier to generate than theory itself. "Theory" remains an elusive category with fuzzy boundaries that involve often hazy adjudications as to what is "theoretical enough," either by level of abstraction ("high theory"), scope of possible generalization ("grand theory"), or as distinguished from "method." Theory is, reciprocally, method-driven; the analytic or interpretive models and questions we are able to pose and test are enabled or restricted by our technologies (and in turn our techniques) of observation. This reciprocity is a particularly obvious dynamic in the case of those theorizations based on close textual analysis of oral performance, all of which were invented subsequent to—and supported by—various modes of audio and visual recording.

Audience and Authority

There is little debate in the articles presented here about the nature of authority in folklore theory. Folklorists seem comfortable with Geertz's claim in 1973 that cultural theory, supported by qualitative research methods, is properly to be considered interpretive, not predictive. Interpretation in this sense is not limited to deciphering or ascribing meanings to entextualized expressions (i.e., content interpretation), but also includes theorizing how expression is accomplished: the full range of observed or posited acts, processes, and inferred appropriateness rules applying to the generation of expressions (the ethnography of performance).

I therefore propose that a major criterion for evaluating interpretive theory (whether high, grand, middle, or humble/low) should be not its power to exclude or preclude the application of other theories to the same or overlapping data sets, but its aptness. One question that must always be asked is thus "explanatory for whom?" *Whose* questions does it answer, generated by what dialogic process? What is the general cultural or prior-theoretical context in which this theoretical/interpretive formulation asserts or identifies otherwise unacknowledged relationships between the expressions under examination, their processes of creation, other cultural formulations, and/or other possible interpretations (meanings)? Evaluations of theory are in part determined by the audience. This audience may include members of the communities participating in the expressive events being theorized about and/or outsiders ("exo-" or "etic" theorists). Aptness may be gauged by competent practitioners (active or passive) of the cultural form or by outsiders who presumably look for patterns not visible or immediately relevant to practitioners. The degree of "emicness" may validate or invalidate a given theory, depending on the epistemological theory, politics, or ethics of the metatheorizer. Note the implicit politics—the implied legitimacy or illegitimacy of a distribution of interpretive authority or power—in a term such as Dundes's "informant intimidation" (2005, 402). Thus, evaluations by competent "informant" practitioners of a given theory's interpretation may serve to evaluate a theory's validity or merely to gauge its distance from emic views. One can imagine at least four informant-audience reactions that indicate degrees and varieties of emic/etic distance, from low, experience-near, or emically close, to emically distant in various ways:

1. "Yes. Right, that is what we do/say/think/mean." ("This may be a translation or a formulation of something we don't usually bother to formulate, but it makes sense to us.")

2. "Yes, well, we can see why *you* see it that way." (cognitive/heuristic hospitality, engageable)

3. "*Wrong!* This doesn't fit our interpretive/appropriateness rules and here's why." (The "you're probably a teachable idiot" response.)

4. "Huh?" (unprocessable difference)

This last reaction will be a tolerable, even desirable, index of theoretical power for exo-theorists (e.g., Marx, Freud), part of whose epistemological/political agenda is to trace or create templates of interpretation not thinkable for the culture bearers, for reasons that then would need to be theorized (the unconscious, false consciousness, deniability/coding, etc.).

Salvaging the heuristic value of an exo-theory that gets the "Huh?" response generally entails some theorizing of why/how the informants/respondents can't or won't think like the theorist. While middle-range, experience-near, low, or "humble" theorizations (see Dorothy Noyes's chapter in this book) could reliably garner the first three responses, grand or high-theory formulations, with less specific grounding to local cases, and/or higher orders of abstraction, are likely to receive the last response, at least on first introduction.

Despite initial resistance from the population to which a theory is applied, a process of "emicization" or vernacularization (more often pejoratively called *vulgarization*, as much, I think, in defense of intellectual hegemonies as of conceptual precision) may then ensue. Emicization processes, involving the selective "grounding" of some but not all key theses or concepts, have been dramatically visible in the case of both Marxist and Freudian theory in twentieth-century Euro-American popular culture and are perhaps now to be observed vis-à-vis theories of globalization. In keeping with folkloristics' core concerns—traditionalization, repeatability with variation, cultural creativity, continuity, and change—processes of selective emicization of "high" or "grand" theory seem ripe for our analysis (dare I say theorization?), together with the equally interesting, often co-existent, phenomenon of theory-resistance to be detected through case studies ("who do you think you're summing up and what business is it of yours?"). Responses of the second and third varieties, variously articulated, may be indicators of such emicization processes.

Theory as Paradigm, Paradigm as Metaphor, and the Idea of Aptness

If qualitative social theory, including folklore theory, is interpretive in nature, then all theory describes something (the data or phenomena theorized about) in terms of something else (ascribed logics, patterns, processes, meanings, values). The interpretive theoretical relationship is closer to metaphor ("It's like X") than prescription ("It is X"). If one takes to heart the principle of the arbitrariness of representation at the level of signs, then the openness of interpretive theory and its non-determining relationship to data become clearer (and perhaps more tolerable). If a theoretical paradigm functions like a metaphor—if it establishes resemblances or parallel features, without precluding the applicability of other paradigms or metaphors to the same phenomena or exhausting the possibilities for how the phenomena are perceived theoretically or experienced generatively—we begin to have a poetics of theory. This idea of aptness within an open, indeterminate system does, however, compromise some basic goals of "high" or "grand" theory, if those goals include precluding other theories. Indeterminacy as defined here is not to be confused with obscurity, lack of transparency, or the difficulty of not being able to identify clearly some grounding data to which a theory can be applied. Aptness, resonance, and suggestive power become criteria of productive theory, rather than exclusiveness, comprehensiveness, or level of abstraction. Aptness itself is, of course, encompassed and enabled by culturally-constructed domains of meaning and association, which takes us back to the question of whose theory. But indeterminacy is no excuse not to do theory. Aptness is persuasive; persuasion is power.

Theories of the Local and Localization

One reason given for the alleged theory-impoverishment of folkloristics is a preference, in research and public presentation, for documenting local expressive culture in a way that too readily adopts, as it celebrates, the practitioners' own sense of their cultural uniqueness. We have long been interested in variation, including local variation (e.g., oicotypification). However, that sense of local uniqueness, if taken at face value, short-circuits comparative higher-level modeling or theorization of the ways in which localization is achieved or maintained, i.e., how the local, as a marker of community identity, is produced, experienced, and sustained. While variation of formal properties and features (types, motifs) has historically been a major concern of folkloristics, there is also a large later body of folkloristic research on performance pertinent to variation in transmission, including localization, as a process. (Space constraints here preclude a

review of that literature, some excellent examples of which are Briggs
1988, Slyomovics 1987, Reynolds 1995, and Goldstein 2004.)

A productively incomplete model of local cultural continuity has
been Pierre Bourdieu's highly influential theorization of *habitus*
(1977). One thing hard to find in Bourdieu's model was a theorization of change in habitus, especially the generation and regeneration
of the local (consciously claimed or not) in dialogue with the non-
local. As Dorothy Noyes points out in this volume, folklorists have
historically been provincial intellectuals, concerned with construct-
ing "a viable whole out of their local realities and the higher order."
A comparative study of such processes of generating the local (the
invention of the nation-state among them) could evaluate case studies in which the local is competitively juxtaposed with different versions of the national, ethnic, or global. One complex array of such
specific local practices in Afghanistan might include:

—rules of reciprocity [both for revenge and hospitality],

—rules of gender and social contact,

—male and female dress, and

—permitted and proscribed verbal performance genres.

Treatments of this particular array of topics have been attached to
different local, ethnic, (perhaps proto-) national, or global (religious) identities or groups, by different local players at different moments in the recent, wickedly contestive cultural politics of that
unfortunate country. That such attachments of practices to group
identities is largely accomplished rhetorically, whether by insiders
or outsiders, assigns this topic unequivocally to the realm of philology
of the vernacular (Richard Bauman's term in this volume) in conversation with the global. Furthermore, our topic could and should
be not only the process of localization, but also its other half, the
entry of the local into the global (Narayan 1993).

I support Richard Bauman's apt designation of our field as the
"philology of the vernacular," with the proviso that there is now, at
least, more overlap than he discusses in both theory and method
between philology's text-focused intellectual legacy and the folklife
movement (for a discussion of the folklife movement by its most
prominent U.S. founder, see Yoder 1990). This relationship deserves
further discussion. Several participants in discussions at AFS brought

up Dell Hymes's definition of our enterprise as centrally concerned with processes of cultural performance, transmission, differentiation, and traditionalizing (1975). To understand these phenomena, we generate and adapt analytical or interpretive frames that assume (and champion) a common humanity beyond the pull of the local or of privilege. Nevertheless, the pull of the local—as well as that of differentiation as hierarchy, of privilege, and of power—remains key to those topics and cases that excite our analytic attention and is central to the dynamism we wish to understand. Logistically, we need to foster styles of interaction (research and presentation, publishing and reading practices) for identifying parallel cases and analyses across boundaries of space, time, and discipline in order to build more scope into our modeling of localization, building on our individual, fine-grained observation and presentation of local communicative acts and systems.

Pragmatics of Theory, from Marginal to Liminal

What is theory for? Is it a tool, with functions? Or a product, with exchange value? Or both? Perhaps thinking of the theme of the 2005 AFS meeting, "Folklore, Equal Access and Social Justice," Dorothy Noyes observed in the discussion that "grand theory purports to be about the world, and not just for fun." If a significant proportion of folklorists were to address that theme, J. L. Austin's understanding of the various possible purposes of a speech (communicative) act would open up the question of critical theory in folkloristics, theory that aims to challenge, and thus to change or to reform the processes, institutions, and mentalities that it reflects on. To do so, it must stand apart from its object, conceptually, and discursively. That distance may be achieved in part by the perceived "height" of the theory (level of abstraction). To be effective as critical theory, however, it must be sufficiently "grounded"—connected to and reflective of the patterns it seeks to critique in a sufficiently obvious manner—to be so perceived by its intended audience. "High" or "grand" theory is "difficult" (intellectually challenging, hard to apply) in proportion to its distance from the emic theory applied to its target phenomena. In the political economy of academic knowledge, the power of "high" or "grand" theory's positioning is measured in part by obscurity—in fact by unequal access: by its reliance on terms of reference that are differentially available to those who are initiated in, and committed to, specialized theoretical discourses developed as professional jargon. Critical theory intended to shape general opinion must therefore address this distance problem and operate at Dorothy Noyes's middle level.

We might wish to distinguish among pragmatic (often self-claimed) political purposes for theory making. These can range from "outing" (exposing the operative relationships of covertly-operating expressive institutions or economies) to "liberating" (foregrounding and, by various tropes, positively valorizing neglected or covert communicative strategies of the disempowered). There is also the (theoretical) possibility of theory for nothing at all, theory for theory's sake, or theory for fun; however, any attempt at shared intellectual control does, I think, have some political implications, however carefully internalized. As an example of these implications, Susan Sontag suggested, from a decidedly modernist, avant-garde standpoint, that interpretation of artistic production could be liberating in the sense of enabling change, redistributing power by "revitalizing" passé works of art. However, as she points out, it can also be reactionary, reductionist, in her view "deadening," taking the form of "the revenge of intellect upon art," some sort of compensation for the theorist's or the hegemonic culture's lack of creative capacity (1969, 3–14).

Meanwhile, the legacy role of folklorists as the professional (or amateur) mourners and memorialists of what nineteenth- and early twentieth-century liberals assumed to be disappearing cultural productions and identities has somehow morphed in two directions, through participation in some notably toxic modes of cultural nationalism (see John W. Roberts's contribution in this volume). First, nonfolklorists continue to view folklorists as reactionary champions of the past and anti-liberal opponents of liberal nationalism (and/or globalization) (Hobsbawm 1990). In contrast, folklorists perceive themselves as champions of cultural democracy—of the viability of minority cultural systems within large national or transnational economies.

We have good reason to engage with theorization, not only of the marginal (not to be assumed synonymous with the disappearing) but also (and alongside) the liminal or liminoid: the cultural positions and expressive activities situated on the edges, not necessarily of cliffs, but of dynamic divides of various kinds. We could usefully contribute to theorizing circumstances in which the marginal becomes the liminal (acquiring brokering roles and powers, as when a traditional artist or artists for better or worse become representatives of a nation or subnational community in an evolving wider cultural economy) and vice versa, when a liminal actor or actors become marginalized.

Disciplinary Identity and Turf Wars

Discussion in the 2005 forum traced the historical capacity of members of our discipline to generate analytic or interpretive strategies identifiable as theory and potentially interesting to other disciplines as well. It then moved to the question of who gets credit for idea-building in an interdisciplinary intellectual climate, as well as how, and to what effect, that credit is given. Historically speaking, key concepts of folklore were framed before its disciplinary boundaries were drawn and these concepts continue to ignore or compromise such boundaries. The discipline (or more accurately, its subject matter, "folklore" in English) was defined 100 years *after* the study of key, discipline-defining categories of data began. As discussion that morning at AFS devolved from history of ideas as disciplinary history into a revisitation of the logistical implications of our ongoing disciplinary identity crisis, significant differences of viewpoint appeared about whether either the subject matter or the theory (styles and goals of analysis/interpretation) *can* effectively define our discipline (even if and as these dimensions change over time). There were voices, both on and off the panel, debating the pros and cons of trying to define and defend disciplinary boundaries and identities at all. Discipline-envy and theory-poaching seem to be a normal part of the political economy of formal knowledge across most or all academic fields; our special problem is more one of critical mass, the small number of our training sites and thus our capacity for self-replication in formal training. Metaphorically, though, we can ask whether our problem is really habitat-loss (there are presently many venues and job titles under which trained folklorists are working) or rather blurred speciation. Debate continues as to the potential effects of individual and collective interdisciplinary mobility and composite identity. To what extent is intellectual vitality the enemy of turf? How much (and what kind of) turf does a discipline or community of thinkers need, to self-replicate, to develop, and to propagate ways we think and things we know how to do? Visibly effective theory-building, including cultural (dare I add, critical?) meta-theory building, helps maintain our productive presence in the academy, which often seems to reduce to a theory-for-theory's-sake zone. The application of that theory in our other sites of endeavor can take many forms and we should strive to make its usefulness visible in and out of the academy.

References

Austin, J. L. 1962. *How to Do Things with Words.* Oxford: Oxford University Press.

Bourdieu, Pierre. 1977. *Outline of a Theory of Practice,* trans. Richard Nice. Cambridge: Cambridge University Press.

Briggs, Charles. 1988. *Competence in Performance: The Creativity of Tradition in Mexicano Verbal Art.* Philadelphia: University of Pennsylvania Press.

Dundes, Alan. 2005. "Folkloristics in the Twenty-First Century (AFS Invited Presidential Plenary Address, 2004)." *Journal of American Folklore* 118 (470): 385–408.

Geertz, Clifford. 1973. *The Interpretation of Cultures.* New York: Basic Books.

Goldstein, Diane. 2004. *Once upon a Virus: AIDS Legends and Vernacular Risk Perception.* Logan: Utah State University Press.

Hobsbawm, Eric. 1990. *Nations and Nationalism Since 1780.* Cambridge: Cambridge University Press.

Hymes, Dell. 1975. "Folklore's Nature and the Sun's Myth." *Journal of American Folklore* 88 (350): 346–69.

Narayan, Kirin. 1993. "Banana Republics and V. I. Degrees: Rethinking Indian Folklore in a Postcolonial World." *Asian Folklore Studies* 52: 177–204.

Reynolds, Dwight F. 1995. *Heroic Poets, Poetic Heroes: The Ethnography of Performance in an Arabic Oral Epic Tradition.* Ithaca, NY: Cornell University Press.

Slyomovics, Susan. 1987. *The Merchant of Art: An Egyptian Hilali Oral Epic Poet in Performance.* Berkeley: University of California Press.

Sontag, Susan. 1969. [1966] *Against Interpretation.* New York: Dell.

Yoder, Don. 1990. "The Folklife Studies Movement." In *Discovering American Folklife,* 25–42. Ann Arbor: UMI Research Press.

MARGARET A. MILLS is Emerita Professor of Persian and Folklore in the Department of Near Eastern Languages and Cultures at the Ohio State University. Her major publications include *Rhetorics and Politics in Afghan Traditional Storytelling* and the coedited *South Asian Folklore: An Encyclopedia.* Her work in progress includes a coauthored, small, dual-language (Persian/English; Pashto/English) Afghan folktale book for distribution in Afghanistan through the ABLE free library project; an oral history of an Afghan family; and a monograph on the figure of the female trickster in Persian-language oral tradition.

Richard Bauman

5 The Philology of the Vernacular

Grand Theory versus Prevailing Theory in American Folklore

IN MY VIEW—and I suspect most contemporary folklorists would agree with me—any effort to proclaim or construct a grand theory for folklore is a misguided enterprise, notwithstanding the prominent role of grand theory in the development of modern social thought, its rhetorical utility in the political economy of discipline building, and the social capital that still somehow accrues to it in some provinces of academe. The rhetoric and intellectual politics surrounding claims to grand or high theory are all too susceptible to a number of stultifying effects: authoritative regimentation of inquiry, universalizing generalization and *a priori* abstraction that flatten out everything interesting about human existence, and banal "it fits" scholarship (here's the theory, here's my case, and it fits). If, though, we take the question before us to be whether American folklore has a grand theory in the sense of a *prevailing* one, I would answer in the affirmative, at the same time acknowledging that American folklore study has been inflected by a range of theories, some of them representing the reactivation of intellectual kinship with long-lost cousins with whom we share intellectual ancestors but whose families moved away from our neighborhood some time ago.

By prevailing theory, I mean (1) a conceptual frame of reference (2) that guides a general, common engagement with a coherent intellectual program, (3) based on a set of premises about society and culture, (4) providing an orienting framework for inquiry, and (5) derived from or aligned to a demonstrable intellectual tradition. I hasten to say that the common ground is not necessarily fully recognized or understood as such by all practitioners, but it is, I think, demonstrable through reflexive, critical intellectual historiography and attunement to basic premises.

If, then, there is a prevailing theory in American folklore, what is it? The best name I can come up with is *the philology of the vernacular.* Space constraints will allow only a stripped-down and summary characterization of the theory in these few pages; a far more extended consideration of many of the points I will offer may be found in a number of works I have coauthored with Charles Briggs (Bauman and Briggs 2003; Briggs and Bauman 1992).

The Philology of the Vernacular

1. What I am calling the philology of the vernacular is, first of all, *text-centered.* I will elaborate further on the nature of textuality below, but for now, suffice it to say that the primary unit of analysis of all philological approaches is the text, that is, a crafted, bounded, internally cohesive and coherent stretch of discourse. For the most part, folklorists have concentrated their attention on markedly entextualized discursive forms, such as narratives, songs, proverbs, riddles, and the like, but have also tended to entextualize (that is, render in textual form) other cultural forms, like "custom," "belief," and "superstition."

2. It is *relativist,* based on the understanding that texts are expressions of and intelligible in terms of the cultures in which they circulate. It holds, that is, that *texts are culturally constituted.* Some adherents—not all—would hold that the flip side is also true: *culture is textually constituted.* The relativist orientation of philology also establishes a frame of reference in which cultures—nations, peoples, tribes, and the like— serve as the social base for the identification of textual corpora, the elucidation of their characteristic features, and their properties. These corpora are then ideologized as cultural heritage and become the touchstones of cultural nationalism.

   Principles 1 and 2, then, taken together, suggest a reciprocal program: if you want to understand a culture, examine its texts, and if you want to comprehend a text, read it in relation to the culture to which it gives expression.

3. Texts have certain conventional properties: *formal, thematic,* and *pragmatic.* The formal properties of texts have to do with how

they are made, their formal constituents and organizing principles, what it is that marks them off from their discursive surround and renders them internally cohesive—in a word, their
poetics. Thematics, by contrast, has to do with the referential or
propositional content of texts, their ways of representing the
world. The pragmatic dimension of texts pertains to their modes
of presentation and use, how they serve as resources for the
accomplishment of social ends. Taken singly or in combination,
these sets of properties serve as criteria for the identification and
differentiations of various orders of texts, that is to say, of *genres*.

4. The formal, thematic, and pragmatic properties of texts help to
make them *memorable, repeatable,* and thus *sharable* and *durable*.
One of the central concerns of philology is the social and temporal circulation of texts. The iteration and reiteration of texts
gives them social currency as part of a collective repertoire.
There is a temporality to this process as well: successive iterations of a text constitute a temporal continuum of intertextually
related cognate texts, a "*tradition*."

5. While texts may thus be seen to be shared within a culture and
to persist through time, they are simultaneously *subject to change*.
From one vantage point, given the basic philological premise that
texts are keyed to culture—or, indeed, that texts *are* culture—it
follows that when culture changes, so too will texts change. Or, to
approach the process from the vantage point of the dynamics of
textual circulation, as adumbrated in point 4, just above, no two
iterations of a text are ever exactly the same; there will inevitably
be a dimension of variation, an intertextual gap between the
successive iterations. As its texts change, so does a culture change.

Taken jointly, points 3, 4, and 5 provide the basis for a further
extension of the intellectual program I have identified as the
philology of the vernacular. At the center of this program is the
dynamic tension between textual persistence or continuity—tradition—on the one hand, and textual change—variation or creativity—on the other. This tension is calibrated in terms of
persistence or change in the formal, thematic, and pragmatic aspects of texts. At various times, and in various approaches (more
on this below), one or another vector (tradition or change) or one
or another set of textual properties (formal, thematic, pragmatic)

may be foregrounded, but always in at least tacit relation to the others.

6. The nature and capacities of texts are closely tied to the *communicative technology* employed in their production, circulation, and reception. For most of the history of folklore as a concept and a field of inquiry, this nexus has been investigated in terms of the human voice as a communicative technology and of the discontinuities and transformations attendant upon the advent of writing, print, and other media. Orality has figured as the touchstone of folklore from the beginning, with "oral" serving as the characterizing adjective in such compounds as "oral tradition," "oral poetry," "oral literature," all of which often stand in as equivalents of the term "folklore."

7. There is a *sociology of textual production, circulation, and reception* in any culture and historical period. For most of the history of folklore, both as concept and as field of study, the sociological aspect that has been of primary concern is the *social stratification of culture*, with the central— often the defining—focus of attention directed to that stratum (usually at or near the bottom) variously termed folk, common, popular, or vernacular. Likewise, the oppositional contrast of orality and literacy may serve to identify the social base of folklore, as in "oral society" or in marked forms such as "preliterate" or "nonliterate." All of these terms, and the sociological frameworks that underpin them, have complex intellectual histories, and all have been ideologized: differentially valued, contested, and mobilized in the service of different interests. There is thus a politics as well as a sociology of textual production, circulation, and reception. "Vernacular" seems to me to be the least ideologically encumbered of the terms, which is why I adopt it here; moreover, the linguistic resonances of the term articulate well with the core foci of philology.

The *vernacular* is a communicative modality characterized by: (1) communicative resources and practices that are acquired informally, in communities of practice, rather than by formal instruction; (2) communicative relations that are immediate, grounded in the interaction order and the lifeworld; and (3) horizons of distribution and circulation that are spatially bounded, by locality or region. The vernacular, furthermore, can only be understood in dynamic relation to the cosmopolitan; they are opposing vectors in a larger communicative field. If the vernacular pulls toward the informal, immediate, locally-grounded, proximal side of the field, the cosmopolitan pulls toward the rationalized, standardized, mediated, wide-reaching, distal side.

Three Inflections of the Philology of the Vernacular

The philology of the vernacular, as the touchstone of American folklore study, has come in three principal guises, all derived from the same intellectual foundations in the eighteenth and nineteenth centuries, in the ideas of such figures as Thomas Blackwell, Robert Wood, Robert Lowth, Johann Gottfried Herder, and the Brothers Grimm. One line, with a generally literary cast—that is, oriented principally to the history of literature and to text-historical approaches—is the Harvard-based enterprise of Francis James Child, George Lyman Kittredge, Stith Thompson, Archer Taylor, and their epigones. In this line of inquiry, persistence is foregrounded, with change generally cast as a degenerative process that distances successive iterations ("versions") of a text ever further from its originary form. The focus of investigation is thematic variation, as discovered by close intertextual comparison; formal and pragmatic considerations figure hardly at all.

A second line, focused primarily on epic composition and oral poetics more generally, is the oral-formulaic theory most strongly identified with Milman Parry and Albert Lord (Foley 1988). Here, the weight of emphasis is on individual compositional creativity in the act of performance, conditioned by the formal constraints of the poetic system, the contextual constraints of the performance situation, and the purported capacities of "oral cultures." At the same time, however, the dynamic of creativity is counterbalanced by the traditionalizing intertextual alignment of each performance to antecedent recountings of "the same story." This line of inquiry, then, attends productively and in equal measure to formal, thematic, and pragmatic aspects of oral poetics.

The third line, no less philological than the others, is the Americanist anthropological tradition of Franz Boas, Edward Sapir, Paul Radin, and Melville Jacobs (Bauman 2003; Briggs and Bauman 1999; Hymes 1981). Boas gave explicit priority to the textual documentation of Native American cultures and his program for the collection and analysis of textual materials still shapes anthropological practice in the United States, especially in linguistic anthropology. In the Americanist tradition, texts constitute data for three principal lines of investigation: culture-historical, as evidence of historical processes such as diffusion, migration, and culture contact; cultural, as reflections— though selected and refracted—of culture; and linguistic, as extended, natural discourse. While thematic concerns are foregrounded in the investigation of texts as projections of culture, there has always been a significant interest in form in the Americanist tradition, and the analysis of form in relation to function and meaning is a prominent concern in Americanist linguistic anthropology.

Now, having suggested—but only suggested—some of the divergent approaches to the philology of the vernacular, it may be useful to acknowledge those sectors of folklore that stem from other intellectual lineages and follow programs derived from different sets of concerns, though they may be convergent with the philology of the vernacular in certain respects. Here, I would identify most of the concerns that are generally captured under the rubric of *folklife*: material culture, folk architecture, custom, belief, superstition, festival, and the like. These fields of study derive largely from the antiquarian foundations of folklore in the seventeenth and nineteenth centuries, basically concerned with the ways of life—still vernacular, but not textual—of people cast as "pre-modern." To be sure, the philological and the antiquarian approaches are often heavily intertwined, but there are important differences as well. A full treatment of these issues lies beyond the scope of this brief essay; Charles Briggs and I have discussed them at length (2003).

Implications and Conclusions

So what? How does the recognition of the philology of the vernacular as the prevailing theory in American folklore scholarship help us in our scholarly work? First, I suggest, it provides a basis on which to confirm and reaffirm that our field has been guided by a coherent, productive, and durable intellectual program, extending from the late-eighteenth century to the present. Second, it provides a big picture against which new directions—structuralism, performance studies, ethnopoetics, intertextuality, hybridity, what have you—may be recognized as new vantage points on enduring concerns, on issues that don't go away, but remain worthy of persistent exploration. By the same token, recognition of our common foundations provides a critical vantage point on the divergent intellectual interests that seem to divide us; indeed, it would seem to offer a critical corrective to what have been, at some times and in some quarters, divisive tendencies within the field. In my view, it is unproductive in the extreme (I don't often put it that politely) for folklorists to issue cranky jeremiads or self-congratulatory rants about how this or that approach "is not folklore" or does not accord with some personal vision of grand theoretical orthodoxy (Dundes 2005), when a bit of careful, critical intellectual historiography suffices to demonstrate the common elements among them. And finally (for now, at least), reflexive awareness of the basic problems that have engaged us and the intellectual program that draws them together, may help us in charting and providing a warrant for future directions and suggesting intellectual alliances on a more informed basis. For example, our long-established interest in orality and literacy as technologies of communication should suggest to us an extension of our investigations into how vernacular texts are affected by the advent of other communicative technologies, such as sound recording or radio, a line of inquiry in which we might make common cause with media scholars. Further more, the enduring concern in the philology of the vernacular with regimes of circulation and the ways in which the production of texts looks back upon prior texts and anticipates future ones provides a suggestive warrant for our engagement with regimes of intellectual property, in dialogue with literary scholars, media scholars, legal scholars, and others. The philology of the vernacular provides a strong leg to stand on in these pursuits.

References

Bauman, Richard. 2003. "Text: Anthropological Aspects." In *International Encyclopedia of Linguistics*, vol. 4, ed. William J. Frawley, 229–30. Oxford: Oxford University Press.

Bauman, Richard, and Charles L. Briggs. 2003. *Voices of Modernity: Language Ideologies and the Politics of Inequality.* Cambridge: Cambridge University Press.

Briggs, Charles L., and Richard Bauman. 1992. "Genre, Intertextuality, and Social Power." *Journal of Linguistic Anthropology* 2: 131–72.

————. 1999. "'The Foundation of All Future Researches': Franz Boas, George Hunt, Native American Texts, and the Construction of Modernity." *American Quarterly* 51 (3): 479–528.

Dundes, Alan. 2005. "Folkloristics in the Twenty-First Century (AFS Invited Presidential Plenary Address, 2004)." *Journal of American Folklore* 118 (470): 385–408.

Foley, John Miles. 1988. *The Theory of Oral Composition: History and Methodology.* Bloomington: Indiana University Press.

Hymes, Dell. 1981. *"In Vain I Tried to Tell You": Essays in Native American Ethnopoetics.* Philadelphia: University of Pennsylvania Press.

RICHARD BAUMAN is Distinguished Professor Emeritus of Folklore and Ethnomusicology, Communication and Culture, and Anthropology at Indiana University Bloomington. His research centers on oral poetics, genre, and performance. Among his recent publications are *Voices of Modernity* (with Charles L. Briggs) and *A World of Others' Words.*

6 Humble Theory

SOME OF YOU will remember the dictionary definition of the word *humble*, as propounded by Charlotte the Spider: "not proud and near the ground" (White 1952). Just as Charlotte found the epithet appropriate to Wilbur the Pig, perhaps we can agree that it is appropriate to folklorists and the kind of theory-making to which we should aspire. We who wear the scarlet F upon our bosoms are perhaps in no position to be proud and for the present I think we should stop worrying about it: we would be better off cultivating shamelessness. If we are proud of anything, to be sure, it is of being near the ground. I enter, therefore, a plea not for grand but for humble theory.

My student Susan Hanson argues that folklorists tend to study on the ground without bothering to theorize it: we focus on apparently more autonomous matters such as genre and group (2008). Perhaps this is not a matter of pride but of an inferiority complex. Without taking on her challenge of understanding folklore's ground, I'd like to talk a bit about the historical and institutional ground that folklorists inhabit and how that might guide our theoretical aspirations. Two issues lie behind the question posed for the AFS forum, "Why is there no grand theory in folkloristics?"

One, as I've suggested, is straightforward status anxiety. We labor under the stigma of the F-word and are constantly either having to explain it away or to invent in its place new euphemisms. Since the latter arise from the desire to flee the stigma rather than an emergent reordering of the discipline, they are doomed to failure.

I have limited faith in collective campaigns for disciplinary respectability. As everyone from Castiglione to Molière to Bourdieu tells us, the quest for social distinction is doomed to undermine itself. I would also remind us that we are not the only discipline suffering from status anxiety. Even political scientists, who occupy a space far higher than we do on the imagined ladder toward transcendent knowledge, characteristically experience what international relations scholar Ned Lebow likes to call "physics envy." In the course of interaction with specialists in international relations over the years, I have discovered that not a few suffer also from folklore envy. Their grand theories having failed to predict such non-negligible matters as the end of the Cold War, they find themselves attracted to disciplines closer to the ground and attuned to contingencies, softer voices, and the constraints of language and history.

Folklorists, likewise, envy actors both below and above us on this stairway to heaven. Closer to the ground than we are the artists and activists who make social life and whose collective labor shapes its forms. We long to be creative writers or makers of the revolution, not parasites upon such endeavors.

On the other side we have theory envy. The theory in question is typically not the grand theory of social science but the high theory of literary studies and philosophy. The latter has more glamour but can also be more resonant to folklorists, for in its poetic or world-making ambitions it mimics the primary symbolic systems we study.[1] Sometimes we throw up our climbing ropes and haul ourselves painfully from the ground of social experience to the heights of, for example, poststructuralism—often hanging by a thread from a cliff rather than finding a secure footing, step by step. I would remind us of our historical position on the slope or, better said, in the middle. The folklorist has characteristically been a provincial intellectual, and while this position has no glamour whatsoever, it's more significant than we think. The nation-state was made stable by the labor of provincial intellectuals trying to integrate their local realities and the overarching order into a viable whole. Today provincial intellectuals are wrestling with globalization. It's a position that poses strong temptations, to which some folklorists in a variety of historical situations have succumbed—hence the stain of the scarlet F—but it's also a position that offers constructive and critical opportunities possessed neither by the top nor the bottom. We need to learn to live with the ambivalence of the middle position.

The second issue we face is the need to map out useful work in the world for the people who call themselves folklorists. Here I feel there is something to be done. So let me stress that while I don't find the notion of grand theory useful to us at this stage in our disciplinary life—or perhaps ever—I am absolutely not refusing theory as such either in general or for folklorists: I am rather trying to define our right relationship to it.

First, we need to recognize the necessary complexity of folkloristic practice. If you will indulge a lapsed Episcopalian, folklore is a trinity, of which the three persons are indivisible. The field cannot theorize without strongly grounded, in-depth ethnography of particulars. The field has no purpose without engagement in the world, trying to understand and amend the social processes that created the F-word and other, far worse stigmas. Practice in the world has no lasting efficacy without theory to clarify its means and ends and make its efforts cumulative. The ethnographer, the practitioner, and the theorist are mutually dependent and mutually constitutive: they cohabit, to different degrees, in singular folklorist bodies. We tend to forget this and too often moralize the differences between these three tasks because historically they have informed three different types of institution: the archive, the public practice, and the academic program. We who are lodged in these institutions acquire their local dispositions and can hardly help knowing where our bread is buttered. But when any of these three labors is neglected, the discipline suffers. We are currently at the end of a long phase of reaction to an earlier overemphasis on theory, when the lures of science and of objectivity tore us painfully from both grounded understandings and the pursuit of social justice. A restored focus on ethnography and practice has resulted in enormously improved ethnography and more successful practice. But the field has paid a price in fragmentation, no longer knowing how to draw intellectual connections between one situation and another. This fragmentation doesn't only impoverish theory per se: it also saps our ability to understand ethnographic particulars and to create coalitions towards practical ends of liberation.

Instead, we need to render unto theory what is due to theory. In part that means getting over our anxiety about reductionism. Thought is reduction. But humble theory recognizes that all our work is essay, in the etymological sense: a trying-out of interpretation, a provisional framing to see how it looks. In the absence of a better alternative, there is much to be said for the Enlightenment project. Science reduces reality in an effort to understand it but it also properly lays itself open to an ongoing process of collective correction and revision. While science as converted into institutional practice has often not lived up to its own ideals, its authority legitimating various kinds of oppression, we can nonetheless recognize that science's own ideology gives us the tools to make this critique and that there is still a qualitative difference in openness to revision between, let's say, evolutionary theory and intelligent design.

While I would like us, in a humble spirit, to reclaim theory, I would not go so far as to look for grand theory. Grand theory constructs for itself grand objects: human nature, the nature of society, and so forth. Folklore does not have the resources to set up in competition with sociology, psychology, or anthropology. Our history has given us a smaller garden to cultivate, but not an infertile one.

We have our scarlet F to think about. Those forms and practices that have historically been labeled as folklore do not reside in dramatically different and distant cultural worlds from that of the labelers. Folklore is the intimate other of modernity, the remnant which can be swept out of sight but not easily disposed of. Dell Hymes and others have long argued that the stone the builders had rejected should become the cornerstone of the human sciences.[2] There is no reason we should not work toward this goal—but we must recognize our immediate practical limitations. Folklore is also the intimate other of the academy. We are there and not going away, but we will continue to make our colleagues uneasy and we are not going to have armies of scholars out saving the world for folklore any time soon—which may be a good thing. Dealing with the residual, the emergent, and the interstitial gives us quite enough ground for the few of us there are to occupy it.

Along with the external constraints on our disciplinary space, our internal intellectual history provides us with a limited but fertile ground to build on. We should remember that the American Folklore Society was founded as an act of resistance to the grand theory of the period: evolutionary biology as it was mistakenly generalized to account for cultural and social difference. Franz Boas's message was that anthropologists were theorizing in advance of the facts, as Sherlock Holmes would say: they did not yet know how to read the particulars of cultural situations. William Wells Newell deliberately brought together Francis James Child and Franz Boas—one looking at the English stock then being celebrated as the apex of cultural evolution, one looking at Native Americans, seen by the anthropologists as savages at the bottom of the ladder. By putting the expressions of both of these groups under the common lens of German philological method (see Richard Bauman's contribution to this discussion in this volume) and by explicitly setting up these two groups along with new immigrants and once-enslaved Africans as the range of subjects whose lore the AFS should examine, Newell was insisting on the common humanity and common historicity of the people whom grand theory had set asunder. Our field was thus at the inauguration of what Jason Baird Jackson has called "the Americanist tendency toward theoretical modesty, grounded in an appreciation of the complexities of history and ethnography located in actual places and times" (2004, 202). This, as the presidential address of Dell Hymes in 1974 strongly reminded us, is a usable past (1975).[3]

For the moment, we are better equipped to criticize grand theory than to build it. At the same time, however, we can continue to address that middle territory between grand theory and local inter-pretation.[4] Performance theory, it's often said, is only method, but method takes us to theory. We begin to think in the act of describing and see particulars in the act of comparing. We need an analytical vocabulary allowing us to move across situations. We cannot leapfrog from the local into transcendent meaning and my political scientist friends are encountering the reverse problem as they try to plummet in the other direction. The questions proper to our field are in the middle of the ladder. They are not Why-questions but How-questions, about the life of forms in society. They are our old topics: transmission, performance, and differentiation. How do forms move across time and space and remain recognizable? How do the people who recur-rently interact in a given situation generate forms in common, and how do those forms work back again upon their makers? How is form marked by voice, such that we can recognize it as folk, or as Cajun, or as mine, or as Other? We have two centuries of scholarship built upon this ground, which in recent years we have neglected badly. Humble it may be, but we have a there there. We have a there *here* and need not go looking to the stars—cosmic or academic—for salvation.

Notes

1. These symbolic systems are, of course, the mode of vernacular theory, which calls on metaphor rather than abstraction to encapsulate and clarify reality.

As Charles Briggs pointed out in the AFS discussion, vernacular theory was the empty chair at our table in this forum. Vernacular theory is more intimately linked to capital-t Theory than we think. Of course postcolonial studies, science studies, and other fields have amply revealed the Eurocentric categories informing supposedly culture-free theoretical formulations, but there is also a positive side to the relationship. Many in the hard sciences, where grand theory is so unproblematized that it need not be named and defended as such, freely recognize the poetic foundations of their thinking and the frequent impetus to scientific discovery from humble metaphor (e.g., Ziman 1991). Closer to home, the new identity-based disciplines have made an explicit point of building academic theory out of vernacular theory (Roberts 1999, 135).

2. This metaphor was invoked by The Remnant, an appropriately named hip-hop group, in their performance at the opening ceremony of the 2005 AFS annual meeting.

3. Naturally this, like all origin myths, must be treated as such: rhetorically useful and unencumbered by inconvenient nuance. John W. Roberts's closer reading of Newell in this volume reveals that American folklore was not as free of the Europeans' nationalism or the anthropologists' evolutionary racism as we would like to think. But like all good constitutions, Newell's initial program for the AFS provides a blueprint for the eventual transcendence of its own historical limitations.

4. In discussion, Gary Alan Fine pointed to Robert K. Merton's "theories of the middle range."

References

Hanson, Susan. 2008. Lyric Suburbia: Performing Community in Worthington, Ohio. PhD diss. Columbus: The Ohio State University.

Hymes, Dell. 1975. "Folklore's Nature and the Sun's Myth." *Journal of American Folklore* 88: 345–369.

Jackson, Jason Baird. 2004. "Recontextualizing Revitalization: Cosmology and Cultural Stability in the Adoption of Peyotism among the Yuchi." In *Reassessing Revitalization: Perspectives from North America and the Pacific Islands*, ed. Michael Harkin, 183–205. Lincoln: University of Nebraska Press.

Roberts, John W. 1999. "'. . . Hidden Right Out in the Open': The Field of Folklore and the Problem of Invisibility." *Journal of American Folklore* 112 (444): 119–39.

White, E. B. 1952. *Charlotte's Web*. New York: Harper.

Ziman, John. 1991. *Reliable Knowledge: An Exploration of the Grounds for Belief in Science*. Cambridge: Cambridge University Press.

DOROTHY NOYES is Professor in the departments of English and Comparative Studies, a faculty associate of the Mershon Center for International Security Studies, and a past director of the Center for Folklore Studies, all at the Ohio State University. Her books include *Fire in the Plaça: Catalan Festival Politics After Franco, Humble Theory:*

Folklore's Grasp on Social Life (IUP, 2016), and the forthcoming *Sustainable Interdisciplinarity: Social Research as Social Process* (with Regina Bendix and Kilian Bizer). A Fellow of the American Folklore Society, she teaches courses in folklore and performance theory, American regional cultures, fairy tale, poetry and politics, the cultural history of trash, and cultural diplomacy.

7 Grand Theory, Nationalism, and American Folklore

DIFFICULT QUESTIONS ABOUT the role of theory in folklore study have often been raised within the history of the discipline. These persistent questions have, at different times, created a great deal of anxiety over issues of theory. This anxiety has manifested itself in attempts to reconcile seemingly disparate approaches. However they have been characterized—as armchair philosopher versus fieldworker, literary versus anthropological, professional versus amateur, academic versus public—these labels and the seemingly dichotomous approaches that they suggest have only served to obscure the state of theoretical development in the field. Moreover, the debates spawned by these different approaches suggest that a divide exists between theory and practice, in ways not experienced in other disciplines. Of the questions consistently raised, the one concerning "grand theory" seems particularly urgent. Alan Dundes suggested that "the continued lack of innovation in what we might term 'grand theory'" is crucial to an understanding of the current state of the discipline in the academy and he claimed that it is the "principal" reason for the decline in folklore programs in universities (2005, 387). He further asserted that this lack has caused folklore to be perceived as a "weak academic discipline" and, in large measure, is responsible for an absence of a level of respect for folklore necessary for its institutionalization in universities (393).

One of the difficulties in responding to questions related to theory in folklore has to do with the intricate relationship between theory and definition. Both have proven to be illusory prizes in the search for clarity in folklore. Various reasons can be offered for the difficulty in defining and developing theoretical models for folklore study.

Grand Theory in Folkloristics (2016); 78–87, DOI: 10.2979/grandtheory.0.0.08

Perhaps none is more cogent than the fact that it is a discipline with
many origin narratives, each of which carries its own history and tradition of engagement with the subject and each of which tends to be
deeply implicated in nationalistic imperatives that inaugurated programs of study in different nations. Of course this recognition is not
new. In his 1946 presidential address to the American Folklore Society,
Melville Herskovits identified nationalism as one of the most important
factors governing efforts to conceptualize the field (92). He cited examples from Germany, Scandinavia, and Latin America to illustrate
nationalistic influences on the definition and conception of the field
and concluded that these different approaches "show clearly how per-
ennial has been the problem of definition and delimitation of the scope
of folklore" (1946, 93). The distinct origin narratives that arose as a
result of nationalist imperatives, though motivated by similar factors,
are neither totally disparate nor unconnected, but their distinctiveness
has rendered a historically situated disciplinary project virtually impossible. Such a project would make it possible to braid together loose
intellectual strands into one continuous, coherent master narrative,
so necessary for the production of grand theory. Of equal importance,
the distinctive origin narratives make it virtually impossible to imagine
approaches to folklore that do not take into account the influence of
nationalism.

American folklorists, however, have often argued that the study of
folklore in America originated as a unique tradition of scholarly
engagement free of any influence from nationalism (Abrahams
1988; Bell 1973). Dan Ben-Amos, for instance, argues that Williams
Wells Newell was able to develop an "American configuration of folklore" without nationalism by asserting that American "regional diversity and multiple ethnicity [sic] have left no space for the popular
nationalistic spirit" (1998, 259). Other folklorists he cites have used
Newell's emphasis on cultural pluralism as evidence of both the novelty
of his approach and of an absence of an American nationalistic imper-
ative for folklore.

Although Newell's inclusion of the traditions of diverse cultural
groups may have represented a novel conception of folklore at the
time, it does not necessarily follow that it was uninfluenced by
nationalism. Some contemporary scholars have advanced a more
expansive view of nationalism to suggest that nationalism had a

profound influence on the initial conception and continuing practice of folklore in the United States. For instance, Margareta Mary
Nikola offers a helpful view when she argues that, "as an ideology
[nationalism] is a form of political expression; as a subjective element
it defines the nature of the relationship of a person to a collectivity"
(1998). If nationalism is characterized not only by a generally accepted
ideological component, but also by a "subjective element" that allows
it to manifest itself as a project dedicated to defining relationships
within a nation, then one is better able to understand a characteristic
of nationalism that has facilitated folklore study around the world.
Within various nations, folklore study was inaugurated to establish a
relationship between groups that came to be represented as folk and
non-folk. Within this configuration, the folk were perceived as the
marginal and seemingly backward segment of a relatively culturally
homogeneous population. Collection and study of vernacular traditions served as a means of providing a cultural and temporal link
between the folk and the non-folk, the latter being a collective of
individuals whose status was accepted as constituting the contemporary center of social existence in the nation.

A difficulty in envisioning nationalism as an influence on the work
of American folklorists derives from our view of it as a force in
American society. Michael Billig suggests that nationalism in the
American context is a "peripheral force" and that "those in established nations—at the centre of things—are led to see nationalism as
the property of others, not of 'us'. . . . Nationalism, far from being an
intermittent mood in established nations, is the endemic condition"
(1995, 6). As an "endemic condition," American nationalism was not
something that Newell could have escaped as he sought to envision
the work of American folklorists. Nor could succeeding generations
of American folklorists avoid nationalism as they worked to establish
folklore in the American academy.

Newell's attempt to develop a paradigm for American folklore
study was influenced by European conceptions of folklore, themselves
deeply implicated in nationalistic movements. One such conception
was the social-evolutionary framework popular for conceptualizing
folkness in European nations, where it had already become a way to
define the relationship of a certain segment of a population to another, based on a perception of active engagement with tradition. The
paradigm Newell developed maintained continuity with the European

scholarly tradition by identifying what he considered the contemporary social center of the nation and what he conceived of as a marginal, backward element that constituted the American folk. Another influence was a nationalist ideology born of the American historical experience. By the late-nineteenth century and in the shadow of the Civil War, a concern with the relationship of various races and ethnicities had already become such a part of the ideological fabric of the country that it overdetermined Newell's emphasis on cultural pluralism as a basis for folklore study in America.

Newell envisioned British descendants in this country as occupying a dramatically different position on the evolutionary ladder than the other groups that he includes in his vision of American folkness. In distinguishing between what he calls "Relics of Old English Folk-Lore" and the "Lore" of various other groups, including African Americans, Native Americans, French Canadians, and Mexicans (1888), his terminological shift from "relics" to "lore" made clear his view that British descendants represented a contemporary and enlightened element in American society within an evolutionary model. Their possession of relics made them not folk, but passive bearers of tradition. He thus argued that the "relics" of Old English folklore in the United States existed as "titillating remains of past traditions sufficient to stimulate, rather than satisfy, curiosity," traditions related to "the quiet past" (5).

Having established British descendants in the United States as the nonfolk element within the society, Newell's argument explained the possession of vernacular traditions by the other ethnic and racial groups in his catalogue as an important element of their difference from Anglo Americans. While he is silent about the status of the French Canadian and Mexican populations as folk, he clearly articulates his view that the cultural and political status of African Americans and Native Americans defined their status as folk. Consistent with his view of folklore as a "fast-vanishing" form of creative cultural production within an evolutionary framework, he identifies their status as a changing one, seeing both groups as being on a fast track toward civilization for different reasons. The recent emancipation of African Americans from slavery serves as a primary impetus for a dramatic cultural change. In the most politically charged statement in his discussion, he notes that African-American freedom has made this group "for good or ill . . . an indissoluble part of the body politic of the

United States" (5). Although he would eventually be forced to defend his decision to include Native Americans as folk, his initial statement on the subject justifies their inclusion based on a similar perception of imminent cultural change. In a veiled reference to the growing reservation system for Native American containment, he asserts that "a great change is about to take place in the condition of the Indian tribes," one that will alter their relationship to the nation by transforming a primitive people into a civilized one. Accordingly the collection of their folklore will provide a record of "what they have been" (6).

Although Newell may not have thought of his musings as either definitive or theoretical, they nevertheless established an influential paradigm for the study of folklore in the United States. Much scholarly work has focused on the collection and study of creative cultural production within discrete groups. Newell also established a line of scholarly investigation, the heart of which lies in the relationship of various groups to the "body politic."

The spirit of nationalism, I suggest, has played an important role in our efforts to define and theorize our enterprise. Historically, our efforts have been neither apolitical nor lacking in influence from imperatives deriving from nationalistic ideologies as they have manifested themselves through American history. It is simply the case that, when we have evoked nationalism as an influence, we have tended to turn it on its head in the way suggested by Billig: American folklorists working in an established nation have tended to see nationalism as the property of those on the periphery rather than those at the center. As such, much of the scholarly engagement with folklore in America has represented attempts to assess the influence of other nationalisms on vernacular creativity among diverse groups. While approaches based on the influence of other nationalisms have not necessarily been wrong-headed in themselves, they have frequently been problematic because they have rested on embedded but unacknowledged political and/or ideological motives derived from the influence of an endemic American nationalism.

Much of the history of folkloristic engagement with African-American folklore, for instance, has been greatly influenced by a concern with nationalism in this peculiar sense. Nationalism as an influence on African American folklore has been viewed historically as either "African" (in a generalized conception of Africa as a place of national origin) or as "African American" (in the sense of a distinct cultural group). From the beginning an exploration of the influence of an African cultural past constituted an appropriate focus for an investigation of African American vernacular traditions, but political motives, all too often unacknowledged, have governed these efforts. Almost immediately, a controversy erupted over whether the African-American vernacular tradition had been influenced by the African past or owed its existence to exposure to European cultural forms. This debate was able to dominate discourse on this tradition for almost a century primarily because it emerged out of, and was continually fueled by, ideological concerns reflecting American nationalistic imperatives rather than concerns that animated African-American cultural life. The debate over African origins persisted because of continuing ideological and political clashes over the implications of people of African descent actually becoming a part of the American nation. Political positions developed to support disparate approaches to questions raised in debates about black integration versus segregation. Along the way, the controversy claimed strange political bedfellows because of the failure to acknowledge its ideological and political underpinnings. That is, the controversy, when examined on its own terms, creates difficulties in determining the socio-political stance of the various scholars who participated because they failed to interrogate the ideological sources of their pronouncements.

One of our most prominent folklorists, the late Richard Dorson, illustrated this difficulty when he denied an African cultural influence on African-American folklore:

> While the Indian met the white man on fairly equal terms in the seventeenth century, and gradually slipped down the social and cultural scale to the position of a frontier savage and a government ward, the Negro has steadily moved upward from slavery. Torn from his West African culture and denied education, the slave commenced life in American bereft of his own institutions and traditions, and barred from those of his master. Yet while the cultural inheritance of the Indian tribes steadily dwindled, the cultural possession of the Negro bondsmen steadily grew. (1959, 166)

Dorson went on to explain this growth by arguing that,

> the Negro from the beginning lived inside the white man's society. Willy-nilly he acquired the tongue of his master, some of his blood, and segments of his culture. The white planter graced the beds of his

slaves and herded them into his churches. The mulatto children and
the shouting congregations that resulted, though denied full and equal
recognition by their progenitors, still tacitly betrayed some degree of
intimacy between the races. (1959, 167)

While today we might be inclined to dismiss this almost slanderous
representation of two cultural groups as simply racist, perhaps sup-
portive of a deeply conservative ideology of race, I would suggest
otherwise. Dorson's statement reflects a liberal American nationalist
sentiment. His writing emerged out of the widely held "melting-
pot" theory of American culture, which held that Americanization
occurred as a result of shedding influence from a previous cultural
heritage so that distinct ethnic and racial groups would blend into
the fabric of American society. Folklorists who subscribed to this view
thought that, by denying the existence of a continuing cultural influence from an African past, they were supporting African-American
aspirations towards full participation in the society. A consequence
of this view, however, was that it complicated efforts to account for
manifestations of African American cultural difference, as reflected in
various creative traditions and everyday life. As a result, the application of the melting-pot theory to African-American folklore fueled the
development of various problematic approaches. African-American
allegiance to unique cultural processes and traditions came to be
viewed as a reflection of either innate racial differences or cultural
pathology rather than as evidence of vital creative energies in African-
American communities. Of course, the problem with the melting-pot
theory was that it was not a theory but rather an ideology, not an
explanatory model but rather an ideal.

My point is not to indict Professor Dorson, but rather to suggest
how an unacknowledged and endemic American nationalism has rendered the study of one folklore tradition in the United States problematic in various ways. In its attempt to make African-American
culture conform to the American ideal dictated by the so-called melting-pot theory rather than interrogate it on its own terms, this project
undermined the very cultural pluralism that many have claimed as the
foundation of American folklore study. This early controversy in the
history of American folklore is profoundly relevant to our ongoing
quandary over issues of definition and theory. The failure of folklorists
in this instance to recognize and acknowledge the ideological underpinnings of their arguments has created not only a problematic

scholarly legacy but also, as Adrienne Lanier Seward has pointed out, a "definitional dilemma" that causes us to be able to respond only haltingly to questions of definition in African-American folklore (Seward 1983, 48).

The failure to develop theoretical models that base American folklore study on cultural pluralism has had deeper consequences than its effect on a singular tradition. One of the most significant consequences is exemplified in the effort to promote a belief that we can have a grand theory in folklore, or that it is desirable to have one. This is precisely the problem with Dundes's assessment of the fate of folklore programs in universities. I would suggest that our commitment to develop what I have referred to elsewhere as "universalist paradigms" (Roberts 1999, 133–35), or what Professor Dundes characterized as grand theory, has contributed to the undermining of folklore's position in the university. In a frenzied attempt to claim scientific rigor for the discipline and in seeking to establish folklore as a legitimate academic discipline in universities, we have over-committed ourselves to an apolitical and atemporal project in an effort to produce grand theories of vernacular creativity.

Clearly, it is no accident that the decline of folklore programs in American universities coincides neatly with the emergence in the academy of fields such as African-American studies, postcolonial studies, and ethnic studies in various configurations. These fields arose fully charged politically and willing to acknowledge their own political and ideological agendas, and they were committed to developing models that recognize and accept cultural pluralism as a basis for their interdisciplinary projects. Since folklore is one of the few fields that has included in its purview the groups whose expressive tradition these new fields sought to theorize, folkloristic insights have frequently been incorporated into these enterprises. But these new fields have often found it difficult to sustain a dialogue with folklore, due to its historic commitment to an apolitical class-based folkness. They have found folklore's efforts to honor this commitment both problematic and troubling, seeing folklore as a discipline more concerned with championing the cause of the marginal than with contesting the cultural and social stereotypes that marginality makes possible in society. As a result folklorists often find their work an object of critique within these new disciplines rather than an accepted contribution to their ongoing efforts to deconstruct and demystify structures that maintain marginality.

Our often-unsuccessful attempts to sustain meaningful exchanges with established disciplines are not necessarily a reflection of a failed disciplinary project, but rather a result of approaching our disciplinary project in terms of other disciplines. Folklore still remains uniquely positioned to contribute to ongoing dialogues about the creative and social dimensions of culture. Our historic commitment to investigate forms of creative cultural production associated with culturally and politically marginal groups has forced us to become sophisticated in our understanding of cultural study as contested terrain in the academy. In pursuing this project, however, we need to become more discriminating in making alliances. Perhaps the lesson of nationalism is that established disciplines, like established nations, will always see the kind of engaged ideological and political commitment that must necessarily animate folklore scholarship as something best pursued on the periphery rather than at the center. If so, our continuing efforts to engage in meaningful interdisciplinary dialogue with them will only be half-heard. Our future efforts might be more productively directed toward establishing dialogue with those disciplines that find themselves struggling with and against an academic culture that continues to see their concerns as peripheral to the real work of academia. We have much to teach them about survival on the academic margins. In turn, we can learn how to accept a more energized and politically engaged stance toward scholarship as our heritage, perhaps our legacy. What is certain is that cultural pluralism continues to be our greatest challenge in defining ourselves as a nation and as citizens in a shrinking world. Folklore can contribute to the dialogue that must ensue in confronting this challenge in productive and meaningful ways.

References

Abrahams, Roger D. 1988. "Rough Sincerities: William Wells Newell and the Discovery of Folklore in Late-19th-Century America." In *Folk Roots, New Roots: Folklore in American Life*, ed. Jane S. Becker and Barbara Franco, 61–75. Lexington, Mass.: Museum of Our National Heritage.

Bell, Michael J. 1973. "William Wells Newell and the Foundation of American Folklore Scholarship." *Journal of the Folklore Institute* 10: 7–22.

Ben-Amos, Dan. 1998. "The Name is the Thing." *Journal of American Folklore* 111 (441): 257–80.

Billig, Michael. 1995. *Banal Nationalism.* London: Sage Publications.

Dorson, Richard M. 1959. *American Folklore.* Chicago: University of Chicago Press.

Dundes, Alan. 2005. "Folkloristics in the Twenty-First Century (AFS Invited Presidential Plenary Address, 2004)." *Journal of American Folklore* 118 (470): 385–408.

Herskovits, Melville. J. 1946. "Folklore after a Hundred Years: A Problem of Redefinition." *Journal of American Folklore* 59: 89–100.

Newell, William Wells. 1888. "On the Field and Work of a *Journal of American Folk-Lore.*" *Journal of American Folklore* 1 (1): 3–7.

Nikola, Margareta Mary. 1998. "False Opposites in Nationalism: An Examination of the Dichotomy of Civic Nationalism and Ethnic Nationalism in Modern Europe." http://www.nationalismproject.org/articles/nikolas/title.html

Roberts, John W. 1999. "'. . . Hidden Right Out in the Open': The Field of Folklore and the Problem of Invisibility." *Journal of American Folklore* 112 (444): 119–39.

Seward, Adrienne Lanier. 1983. "The Legacy of Early Afro-American Folklore Scholarship." In *Handbook of American Folklore,* ed. Richard M. Dorson, 48–56. Bloomington: Indiana University Press.

JOHN W. ROBERTS is dean of the college of Liberal Arts and Social Sciences and Professor of English at the University of Houston. Previously he held positions as Professor of English and Dean of Arts at the Ohio State University in Columbus. His research interests center around African-American folklore, especially its place in the history of American folklore scholarship.

8   There Is No Grand Theory in Germany, and for Good Reason

THERE IS NO single, functioning "grand theory" of folklore in the German-speaking world. To a very large degree, present instructional and research practices represent a reaction to, and rejection of, one particular theory for folklore in this part of Europe. It took a world war, a monumental student revolt, and sweeping university reform for scholars in the discipline to rid themselves, rather dramatically, of the very concept of an overarching and inclusive theory. A formal "farewell" was taken in 1970 with the publication of the polemical *Abschied vom Volksleben* (Geiger, Jeggle, and Korff 1970) and a brief two-sentence formula, called simply the "Falkenstein Formula," which says: "*Volkskunde* analyzes the transmission of cultural values (including their causes and the processes which accompany them) in their objective and subjective form. The goal is to contribute to solving socio-cultural problems" (Brückner 1971, 303). In the process the term *Volkskunde*, as well as its use in the title of university departments, has for the most part been abandoned, along with any semblance of a grand theory.

There was, of course, good reason for this leave-taking from any sort of overarching theory. When we look to the past, we find that there was in fact a grand theory *before* there was a study of folklore. Herder theorized that the *Volk* (by which he primarily meant the peasant folk) represented higher individuals who had kept alive the creative spark of their heritage. From that time in the late eighteenth century, until well past the middle of the twentieth century, scholars in Germany, Austria, and Switzerland theorized about the continuity of German traditions among the Volk from some prehistoric time in antiquity down to the present. The theory was refined, but never really changed. The work of the Grimms, for example, placed *Germany* at the center of the Indo-Germanic (their term for Indo-European) continuum, resulting in what we now refer to as the Indo-European hypothesis and the broken-down myth theory, both of which were quite long-lived and influential far beyond the linguistic boundaries of the German world. One need only read the introductions to the various editions of *Household Tales* to see that the Grimms also thought of German peasants as the keepers of "a belief dating back to the most ancient times, in which spiritual things are expressed in a figurative manner" (Thompson 1946, 369). There is a certain irony here, since the Grimms themselves never went directly to the German Volk for their stories, but collected mostly from an educated middle class. In the early part of the twentieth century, folklorists from the German-language homeland successfully rejected emerging theories, such as those of psychoanalysts Sigmund Freud and Carl Gustav Jung, as well as those from abroad, particularly from Russia. Neither the structural studies by Vladimir Propp nor the interest in the "narrator complex" by Mark Azadowskii resulted in theories that were adopted and employed to any degree. The Swiss Eduard Hoffmann-Krayer merely enhanced the peasant theory with his concept of a *vulgus in populo,* and his postulate: "The folk soul does not produce, *it reproduces*" (1903 [1958], 70), emphasis added). Hans Naumann's *gesunkenes Kulturgut* did little more than trace folk materials that are "produced in upper classes [of society]," from where they "sink down" to "lower classes" of the community (1921, 1). Attempts to add concepts of a *Volksseele* (folk soul) or a *Volksgeist* (folk spirit) never really challenged the centrality of peasant folk culture to the study of folklore.

The years of National Socialism in the German Reich allowed a decidedly fascist discipline to add race and nation to the theoretical mixture of peasant culture, one "based on blood and race as the tradition-bearing and formative powers of the folk-nation" (Ziegler 1934). Folklorists in Vienna, such as Richard Wolfram, Otto Höfler, and Georg Hüsing, all put forth unique but aberrant myth-ritual theories that had virtually no impact beyond Austria (indeed scarcely beyond Vienna). These theories nevertheless concentrated also on the German Volk of prehistorical times and the remnants of their myths and rituals in modern-day practices.

In the early postwar years there were so many oppressive problems from the immediate past that most scholars simply fled into the present, but there were clear indications that the grand theory of the past was still very much alive and well. In 1970, Richard Wolfram called for "structured insights" (*gestalthaftes Sehen*), a term which he never really clarifies. Leopold Schmidt, also from Vienna, tried to influence the postwar discourse with an attempt to re-define Volkskunde as the scholarship of "life according to traditional orders" (*Leben in überlieferten Ordnungen*) and the beginning of an "epoch of objectivity" (1947, 119, 121, 123), but his theory was little more than a rephrasing of folklore from the past. In fairness, there are signs of Schmidt's interest beyond the traditional folk, but his publications are overwhelmingly devoted to Austria's rural populace. When Richard Weiss's *Folklore of Switzerland* appeared immediately after the war in 1946 it seemed to be an irreproachable document from neutral territory and was written in an elevated style of language. Still, it too offered little change in its emphasis on peasant culture and continuity with the past. Finally, a completely new area of scholarship developed in the immediate postwar era as a result of the displacement of millions of ethnic Germans: the study of the folklore of those "driven from their homelands" (*Heimatvertriebene*), particularly from the East and the Balkans. The fate of other refugees—those who survived the concentration camps and the hordes of displaced persons—was, however, not treated by folklorists, who focused only on the Heimatvertriebene. This research, too, remained in the ambit of "German folklore" and differed little from the grand theory of the past, the continuity of traditions among German peasants (Dow 2004).

During the Adenauer years, when the functioning slogan for almost all of life in Germany was "no experiments," university courses and accompanying research were limited to the tried and true. In this way, German society supported a continuation of emphasis in folklore studies on the peasant, now more often referred to as "rural" folk. Even so, in hindsight we are aware that there was in fact slow movement away from what might be called the German *Sonderweg*, that "romantic and national version of cultural history with . . . a social-sciences orientation," as the historian Thomas Nipperdey described Volkskunde (1976, 42). Essential to this new direction was the replacement of its philological orientation with social and behavioral scholarship. Statistics and political science were incorporated and there was more emphasis on experience-based studies.

Gottfried Korff[1] describes three intellectual currents that helped German scholars move beyond their singular theory of the past:

First, he describes the positivism debate, lead by Theodor Adorno and Karl Popper among others, on experienced-based methods and the resulting rationalization of research. In brief, "if the theory of society has the obligation to put the cognitive value of phenomena in a critical perspective, then empirical research has the reverse obligation to guard the concept of intrinsic laws from mythologization" (Adorno 1969, 99).

Second, Korff points to the deconventionalization of culture during the 1970s. The educational reforms at the universities in Germany during this time were attached to a new and more democratic interest in "culture for everyone." Thus, folklore scholarship could make a case for its usefulness and relevance for society and it could maintain a commitment to enlightenment. The hoped-for result was a new problem-solving scholarship that would help reverse external conceptions of folklore as interested only in the banal, cute, or insignificant. For example, sociolinguistic studies of language quickly revealed social inequalities associated with dialects.

Third, Korff points to opposition to the "fabricated inwardness" of Germans and Austrians, the unspoken guilty conscience of the Adenauer era. With the broadening of the concept and the legitimization of all forms of culture that make up everyday life, there was the possibility for a long-overdue liberation from elitist and authoritarian dominance, including ivory-tower research. Attacking fabricated inwardness meant distancing oneself from the method used in the 1950s and 1960s to deal with the past by repressing and forgetting it.

The result was a new orientation, or, more accurately stated, a set of new orientations which reflect the work of Volkskunde during the 1980s and 1990s. First, there was a new emphasis on the *sociology of communication and language.* Here German scholars developed basic tenets, procedures, and case analyses to deal with both the historical and current role of popular literature and with mass-media genres. Rudolf Schenda's post-doctoral habilitation set the standard for the study of popular literature in Europe, not just Germany (1970). Second, *community studies* were now undertaken, of a cultural unit, a village, or a small community. In contrast to the *Lebenskreis* (life circle) or *Kulturkreis* (cultural circle) of the past, the emphasis here was on the "civilizing process." In Utz Jeggle's study of the Swabian village of Kiebingen in 1977, the socio-cultural structures for interaction between rituals, customs, and cognitive structures of the inhabitants were the focus of the research. Finally, interest developed in the *study of historical and contemporary everyday culture* and the insightful work of Hermann Bausinger on "functional equivalents" (cited in Korff 1996, 24). In his work, pop songs replace folksongs as the object of research, bestsellers replace fairytales, and housing types replace vernacular farmhouses.

What the historian Hans Ulrich Wehler once described as "antiquarian and amorphous" scholarship (cited in Korff 1996, 25) had made a sociological turn toward life and a vigorous interest in cultural-historical processes. With time there was an easing of the polarity between quantitative and qualitative methods during the 1970s and 1980s, and a pluralism of method and research areas resulted. A single example suffices. Virtually all departments in all of the German-speaking countries now include extensive research on women, both in historical and contemporary contexts.

This article has thus far put a relatively positive stamp on scholarship at German-language universities, but there is reason for concern. There are hundreds, indeed thousands of students who are currently studying what is now almost universally called European ethnology, even though they must compete for employment with students from other disciplines, like history, literary studies, sociolinguistics, and sociology, that have also refocused toward "cultural studies." It is important to note here that no new departments have opened, either in the new states of Germany that came with the reunification in 1990, or in the former states of the Federal Republic of Germany. Austria may in the foreseeable future have only one remaining program, and Switzerland is not immune, as is apparent in the failure to fill the position occupied in Zürich by Rudolf Schenda after his death in 2000.

Far more troublesome, however, is the question of content in the courses and the publications of contemporary practitioners of the discipline. The virtual rejection of a grand theory and the opening up of new research areas, as described above, have resulted in diffuseness in place of problem-oriented ideas, dispersion instead of a broadened concept of culture. The result, clearly noticeable at the biennial meetings of the German Folklore Society, is a kind of *Kulturalismus* and sometimes an annoyingly naive empiricism. The rejection of a grand theory, however troublesome it was, has led to a kind of dilettantism in the name of a broader understanding of culture: "it delights in sniffing at banalities and peculiarities, historical as well as current, while hardly being interested in their genesis and function" (Korff 1996, 27). Among older scholars of the discipline, many of whom are now retired, one often hears that younger scholars are not only uninformed about the history of folklore scholarship, but they are also fundamentally *uninterested*.

A recent suggestion, which would not engender a new grand theory, but would at least place some parameters on the discipline, is to keep empirical cultural studies within its historical folkloristic boundaries and to try to clarify phenomena of traditional folk culture and their observable reactivations in contemporary society. In 1993, at the meeting of German folklorists in Passau, I sat in many sessions with (and interpreted for) Alan Dundes and heard him ask repeatedly, "Where's the folklore?" At present historians and literary critics do a better job of analyzing popular piety, fairytales, and iconography than do folklorists/ethnologists. There are significant research areas within the traditional canon that have not been adequately completed. In particular that portion of the initial grand theory that deals with matters of continuity and persistence deserves more treatment. In addition the matter of collective memory found in rituals, liturgies, and mentalities still requires thought and research. But these core concepts have become a *quantité négligeable*, or more crudely stated, they are "out of discourse." Finally, there is a reason to be concerned that the divergence of forces and the incessant discussions about the renaming process of the discipline bear a shadowy resemblance to the Nazi past in German Volkskunde, when unity and fusion were primary, a most dangerous "grand theory."

Note

1. I have used many of the ideas presented by Gottfried Korff (Tübingen) in an article in *Europæa: Journal of the Europeanists* in 1996. While writing this article, I went to Tübingen and sat with Korff for more than three hours discussing his description of the current situation in German folklore scholarship. He graciously agreed to read and comment on my summary of "Grand Theory," and I would like to thank him for his assistance in preparing this statement.

References

Adorno, Theodor W. 1969. "Soziologie und empirische Forschung." In *Der Positivismusstreit in der deutschen Soziologie,* ed. Frank Benseler, 81–101. Luchterhand: Neuwied.

Brückner, Wolfgang, ed. 1971. *Falkensteiner Protokolle.* Frankfurt am Main: Universitätsverlag.

Dow, James R. 2004. "'Jugenheim 1951' und der Nationalsozialismus. Zur Aktualität damaliger Perspektiven einer neuen Volkskunde." *Jahrbuch für Volkskunde* 27: 7–22.

Geiger, Klaus, Utz Jeggle, and Gottfried Korff, eds. 1970. *Abschied vom Volksleben.* Untersuchungen des Ludwig-Uhland-Instituts der Universität Tübingen 27. Tübingen: Universität Tübingen.

Hoffmann-Krayer, Eduard. 1958. [1903] "Naturgesetz im Volksleben," *Hessische Blätter für Volkskunde* 2: 57–67 [reprinted in Lutz 1958].

Jeggle, Utz. 1977. *Kiebingen. Eine Heimatgeschichte. Zum Prozess der Zivilisation in einem schwä-bischen Dorf.* Tübingen: Tübingen Vereinigung für Volkskunde.

Korff, Gottfried. 1996. "Change of Name as a Change of Paradigm. The Renaming of Folklore Studies Departments at German Universities as an Attempt at 'Denationalization.'" *Europæa: Journal of the Europeanists* 2 (2): 9–32.

Lixfeld, Hannjost, and James R. Dow. 1994. *Folklore and Fascism.* Bloomington: Indiana University Press.

Lutz, Gerhard, ed. 1958. *Volkskunde: Ein Handbuch zur Geschichte ihrer Probleme.* Berlin: Erich Schmidt Verlag.

Naumann, Hans. 1921. "Deutsche Volkskunde." *Deutsche Pfeiler* July: 1–11.

Nipperdey, Thomas. 1976. "Die anthropologische Dimension der Geschichtswissenschaft," in *Gesellschaft, Kultur, Theorie: Gesammelte Aufsätze zur neueren Geschichte,* 33–58. Göttingen: Vandehoeck und Ruprecht.

Schenda, Rudolf. 1970. *Volk ohne Buch. Studien zur Sozialgeschichte der populären Lesestoffe 1770–1910.* Frankfurt: V. Klostermann.

Schmidt, Leopold. 1947. "Die Volkskunde als Geisteswissenschaft." *Mitteilungen der ÖsterreichischenGesellschaft für Anthropologie, Ethnologie und Prähistorie* 73–77: 115–37.

Thompson, Stith. 1946. *The Folktale.* New York, Chicago, San Francisco, Toronto and London: Holt, Rinehart and Winston.

Weiss, Richard. 1946. *Volkskunde der Schweiz.* Erlenbach-Zürich: E. Rentsch.

Wolfram, Richard. 1970. "Plädoyer für gestalthaftes Sehen." *Zeitschrift für Volkskunde* 66: 28–32.

Ziegler, Matthes. 1934. "Volkskunde auf rassischer Grundlage." *Nationalsozialistische Monatshefte* 5 (53): 711–17. (Translated and reprinted in Lixfeld and Dow 1994:188–89).

JAMES R. DOW is Professor Emeritus of German Folklore and Linguistics at Iowa State University. His many books include *German Volkskunde, The Nazification of an Academic Discipline,* and *The Study of European Ethnology in Austria.* He edited the *Internationale Volkskundliche Bibliographie* for ten years and is a senior bibliographer for the Modern Language Association. His folklore articles have appeared in such journals as *Journal of American Folklore, Journal of the Folklore Institute, Asian Folklore Studies,* and *International Folklore Review.*

Comments

9 What Theory Is

Gray, my dear friend, are all theories, And green the golden tree of life.

— Goethe

LET US BE clear about clarification. Wittgenstein once wrote that for him clarity is an end in itself, and his work generally confirms his persistent pursuit of this end (1998, 9e). Anyone who pauses for a moment over this stance will realize the almost pathological deviance of Wittgenstein from academic norms. Seeking clarity is not deviant, but seeking it for its own sake certainly is. As I survey my own work over recent decades, it is apparent that I have engaged in clarification of both concepts and verbal expressions in nearly everything I have written. Though I may have pushed this clarification further than some other scholars, it was nothing out of the ordinary. Occasionally too pedantic, as in my bachelor of philosophy thesis "On Persuading" at Oxford (1954), and often rather too pedestrian for learned colleagues, but never deviant. But it is also apparent that the primary aim of everything I have written has been exposition, advocacy, or critique, and that clarification has served these aims rather than being pursued for its own sake (see introduction in Garver 2006). Whether in the sciences or the humanities, clarity is normally sought for some further end or purpose, rather than as an end in itself.

When readers find Wittgenstein difficult to understand, it is not because of unusual words, or technical terminology, or long and complex sentences, for he avoids those familiar obstacles. It is rather that they do not see what his point is, for he does not seem to be either expounding texts or advocating or rebutting theses. I believe it is correct that he is rarely engaged in those common academic pursuits. For example, he begins his *Philosophical Investigations* (2001 [1953]) with a quotation from Augustine, saying that this passage reminds him of certain things he would like to get clear about. He does not explain the passage either in itself or in the context of Augustine's thought, he does not rebut the thesis of the passage, nor does he endorse it—and after less than half a page, the details of the passage are left aside and Wittgenstein sets out to clarify what he finds puzzling. I cannot imagine that I could begin a paper that way and have it accepted in any peer-reviewed journal. It is from the perspective of a student of Wittgenstein that I come to the questions about theory.

The word *theory* has such varied uses that a lexicographer must have a difficult time noting all the nuances. A theory can be nothing more than a hunch, in which case it may lack not only proof but also any reasonable basis in fact or probability. On the other hand, Newton's Theory of Motion, Einstein's Theory of Special Relativity, Darwin's Theory of Evolution, and Heisenberg's Theory of Indeterminacy are all accepted as scientific achievements. That they are scientific achievements does not entail that they are beyond criticism, but they are certainly recognized as far more than mere hunches. How can we make sense of what theory is or is supposed to be?

When I have sought to clarify what theory is, in the course of teaching and writing, it has generally been in the context of exposition, particularly exposition of different aspects of science. One familiar contrast is between *fact* and theory, but the word *fact* also comes with a great deal of baggage and I find this familiar contrast more suited to polemics than to clarification. In explaining what science is, I find it more useful to follow N. R. Campbell[1] in using the three-fold contrast of *data, laws,* and *theories.*

Data are the plain facts recorded in the course of careful observation, often with the help of instruments. One of the heroes of scientific observation is Tycho Brahe, who constructed a telescope on the Island of Hveen and over the course of some decades recorded the positions of planets relative to fixed stars. He had, of course, some hypotheses, best forgotten, but it is the raw data bequeathed to Kepler that earn him an honored place in the history of science.[2] Kepler's contributions to the history of science are three laws of planetary motion. In each case the laws are universal statements pertaining to the correlation of observed data. The first is that each planet moves in an ellipse around the sun, with the sun at one focus. At first glance this "law" seems simply a description of the course of planets in their orbits. But the orbit of a planet is not directly observable. What Tycho observed were the positions on successive nights. But the description of the orbit is not another observation report but rather a law or rule correlating discrete observation reports. This is even more obviously the case with Kepler's second law—that each planet sweeps out equal areas in equal times, an apparent description that really correlates distinct observations by means of an invariable rule.

Kepler's laws, like those of Galileo about freely-falling bodies and of Huygens about centrifugal force, are more descriptive than explanatory.[3] Newton stood on the shoulders of these three giants to see a bit farther. Newton is credited with "laws of motion" that apply to all three circumstances: falling bodies, planets in their orbits, and objects swung around a fixed point on a string. The important point is that Newton presented not just laws but a *theory*. Newton did not merely describe motion but explained *why* things move as they do and *why* the laws of Galileo, Kepler, and Huygens have to be as they are.

There are two aspects of Newton's contribution that stand out. First, his "laws" have to do with unobservable and ontologically problematic entities—force and gravity. Force and gravity are theoretical rather than empirical entities: there is no way that Tycho Brahe could have observed them the way he observed the apparent positions of the planets. It is characteristic of theory in this sense to explain empirical regularities in terms of non-empirical theoretical entities. Nearly all the key concepts of twentieth-century physics[4] refer to theoretical rather than empirical entities. Second, Newton's laws of motion and theory of gravity are unifying as well as explanatory, showing that what appeared to be the separate and unrelated achievements of Galileo, Kepler, and Huygens are all special cases of the same general laws. That is to say, if you start with Newton's laws of motion and introduce the circumstances studied by Kepler as initial conditions, you can deduce the laws found by Kepler as theorems. In this way, Newton's theory explains the laws of his predecessors.

Philosophers rightly focus their primary attention on the epistemic and ontological dimensions of Newton's theory, but there is a heuristic dimension as well. Newton's achievements provided the framework for both philosophic thought and scientific research for centuries, as quantum theory and indeterminacy do in our day. One of the best examples of this heuristic dimension concerns the gas laws, with respect to which the Kinetic Theory reinterpreted the key concepts of *pressure* and *temperature* in terms of the velocity of molecules and the frequency of their colliding with one another. The heuristic dimension of theory nurtures hypothesis and research rather than knowledge and explanation.[5]

Recent decades have seen various sorts of "theory" used a great deal in social science and in the humanities, generally with the intention of seeking explanatory power. In these fields nuances appear that are largely absent from theories in physics. Explanations by historians and sociologists attempt to say why what has happened *had* to happen. By relying on necessity they are unavoidably theoretical since the events themselves are always just plain facts—accidents, as the philosophers say. In history and in politics, for example, explanations invariably shift the weight of praise and blame. Consider the U.S. Civil War. One school says that it was caused by Southern secessionists, another that it was caused by Northern abolitionists, and a third that it resulted from historic forces that were both irresistible and irreconcilable. Each school rests on a theory, in the sense of insisting on an account of the facts that goes beyond the facts themselves, and each obviously shifts responsibility onto or off of different shoulders. Is there a way of resolving the dispute among these three theories? In reading the advocates of one or another of these schools one can often sense moments of deeper understanding, hinting at the sort of deeper understanding achieved by Newton and Einstein. The hint is vague, however, and the hope is in vain. There is no decision procedure for historical or sociological theories, partly because of the vagueness of the underlying theories but mostly because assessing human responsibility, which looms so large here, does not come into play when evaluating scientific theories.

Literary theory, such as has grown up around the work of Jacques Derrida, makes use of the moralism of historical theory, but its focus is on language rather than on events. Language involves regularities (and irregularities, of course) between words and meanings, regularities and patterns that became much easier to describe in the light of the methods invented by Saussure to describe the phonemes of languages. The patterns and regularities generally appear random or arbitrary. Literary theory, speaking broadly (and perhaps oversimplifying), seeks to explain them in terms of social and cultural forces that remain generally unnoticed. In that way, literary theory (like its analogue, legal theory) often becomes an instrument of the counter-culture, a tool with which to *epâter les bourgeois.*

The paradigm theories of physics provide an overview that frames definitions and delimits the field of research. Theories in the exact sciences are necessarily restrictive because of such definitions and delimitations. These restrictions are needed as a basis for the predictions and experiments on which scientific progress depends. Once we move away from the exact sciences, however, it is no longer clear how we benefit from analytic definitions and firm delimitations. Definitions can even be counterproductive, especially in the case of basic concepts. Unity is not a basic concept in physics, limited mainly to counting and measurement, but it may be central in cultural contexts. The mission of Jesus, for example, is reported to have been to gather into one the children of God who are scattered abroad (John 11, 51–52), but those of his followers who have attempted to define and delimit in order to achieve this (through doctrine, ritual, or ecclesiastical hierarchy) have divided rather than united the professed followers. The crux of the problem is that *any* criterion for membership or inclusion simultaneously serves as a criterion for exclusion. So the overall perspective on unity will need to allow— perhaps encourage—diversity. Is this possible? Paul Anderson (2005), in a response to John Paul II's encyclical on this topic, *Ut Unum Sint* (1995), suggests that it is possible, but only if we avoid definition and delimitation with respect to key concepts. Instead of defining key concepts and specifying criteria, the alternative is to raise up the center through paradigms and contrasts. Paradigms and contrasts can clarify without setting limits, and the concepts that are introduced and clarified by means of paradigms and contrasts can serve as the core concepts of a theory. In many cases they may serve better than concepts introduced by means of definitions and criteria. If that works with respect to the idea of Christian unity, might it also work in folkloristics? Would it amount to a kind of *grand theory?* What might it be good for?

Theories are too varied to come under any single rubric. Perhaps all of them carry us somehow beyond what is right under our noses and perhaps that itself is what's important. But note the great variety.

Some theories count as knowledge while others contrast with knowledge; some theories are testable while others are in principle immune to test; some theories bring understanding while others bring mystery; some theories are calls to action while others concern only ideas, and so on. Given this variety, I do not see how to make a case for or against theory in folkloristics. It is, however, possible and important to make a case for praising the accurate description of facts and the accumulation of reliable data, as was done in physics by Brahe and Michelson and in linguistics by Saussure and Pike. However tempting theory becomes, I have no doubt that those who produce accurate records and descriptions will remain among the heroes of folkloristics.

Notes

1. Norman Campbell flourished at the beginning of the twentieth century, dominating the field with his tome *Physics: The Elements* (1920). After the First World War he participated in the Workers' Educational Association, which offered university courses to union members in evenings. From this work he published his great contribution of popular science, *What is Science?*, and it is from this work that I draw the following material.

2. Another scholar whose principal contribution was carefully observed data is Albert Michelson, the first American to win the Nobel Prize in physics. Michelson is best known for the Michelson-Morley experiment about the "luminiferous ether" that was supposed to carry light from here to there, but the prize was mainly for his earlier descriptive work on refraction.

3. Although primarily descriptive, these laws can also be said to explain how things move, so the contrast between description and explanation is not hard and fast. What they do not explain is *why* things move the way they do, and that is what I mean by saying that they are less explanatory.

4. Not only physics. A key concept in twentieth-century linguistics is that of the *phoneme*, introduced by Ferdinand de Saussure. Phonemes have a quasitheoretical status: they are empirical, since they are part of everyday experience, but they lack material reality (and hence are not recognized by Chomsky). Pike (1947) stresses the methodological over the metaphysical in the contrast between the *emic* and the *etic*, but the eerie combination of theory and direct experience remains.

5. Lee Haring, in his contribution to this volume, notes that the heuristic dimension is a primary motivation for the promotion of "grand theory" by Talcott Parsons.

References

Anderson, Paul. 2005. "Petrine Ministry and Christocracy." *One in Christ* 40 (1): 3–39.

Campbell, Norman. 1920. *Physics: The Elements*. Cambridge: Cambridge University Press.

———. 1953. *What Is Science?* New York: Dover.

Garver, Newton. 1954. On Persuading. B. Phil. thesis, Oxford University.

———. 2006. *Wittgenstein & Approaches to Clarity.* Amherst, N.Y.: Humanity Books.

Goethe, Johann Wolfgang von. 1955. [1903] *Faust,* Part I, trans. Alice Raphael. New York: Rinehart.

Ioannes Paulus PP II. 1995. Encyclical Letter, May 25, *Ut Unum Sint: The Commitment to Ecumenism.* Rome: Vatican Council.

Pike, Kenneth. 1947. *Phonemics: A Technique for Reducing Language to Writing.* Ann Arbor: University of Michigan Press.

Wittgenstein, Ludwig. 1998. *Culture and Value.* 2nd ed. Edited by Alois Pichler, trans. Peter Winch. Oxford: Blackwell.

———. 2001. [1953] *Philosophical Investigations.* 3rd ed. Edited and translated by Elizabeth Anscombe. Oxford: Blackwell.

NEWTON GARVER (1928–2014) was Distinguished Service Professor at the State University of New York at Buffalo. He received his PhD from Cornell University. His career included four books, some seventy articles, two dozen reviews, papers at more than fifty annual meetings of various professional societies, and invited lectures at more than sixty colleges and universities in the USA and a dozen other countries. His last two books were *Wittgenstein & Approaches to Clarity* (2006) and *Limits to Power: Some Friendly Reminders* (2nd edition 2007).

10   Weak Theory in an Unfinished World

I'VE BEEN WRITING ethnography in the U.S. for almost thirty years. This has been a slow, and also sometimes sudden, accretion of modes of attunement and attachment. A kind of attending to the textures and rhythms of forms of living as they are being composed and suffered in social and cultural poesis. A noticing that gropes from a haptic space in the middle of things. The objects of such a practice are things noted obliquely, as if out of the corner of the eye, but also, often, as punctums or punctures. Things that have impact. Things caught in a circuit of action and reaction. Not simple or self-contained things, but things like the way the senses literally jump in moments of spacing out or ducking for cover, or the sad sagging of trajectories that held promise just a minute ago, or the serial build-up of the sense of being *in* one thing and then another, or all the disappearing acts people perform in search of escape or rest or the perfect life.

The perspective I find I have developed over these years and in these practices of attending and attuning to things is akin to what Eve Sedgwick calls "weak theory" (1997). Theory that comes unstuck from its own line of thought to follow the objects it encounters, or becomes undone by its attention to things that don't just *add up* but take on a life of their own as problems for thought. She calls this "reparative" theory—a good thing—in contrast to a "paranoid" or "strong" theory that defends itself against the puncturing of its dream of a perfect parallelism between the analytic subject, her concept, and the world—a kind of razed earth for academic conversation.

Something like this "weak theory" has become a habit for me not only in intellectual practice but also in the structured seductions and perceptions of ordinary life. And not just for me. People are always saying to me "Don't get me started; I could write a book." What they mean is that they *couldn't* and they wouldn't *want* to. Wouldn't know where to start and how to stop. They have stories, tangles of associations, accrued layers of impact and reaction. What a life adds up to is a *problem* and an open question. "Don't get me started," they say. "I could write a book." It would be a book of singularities that don't add up but are always *threatening* to. What people mean by a life—as in "get a life"—is always something about getting yourself *into* something or getting yourself *out of* something you've gotten yourself into and then on to the next thing (if you're lucky). It's a mode of production through which something that feels like something throws itself together. An opening onto a *something*, it maps a thicket of connections between vague yet forceful and affecting elements.

As Wallace Stevens writes in "July Mountain,"

We live in a constellation
Of patches and pitches,
Not in a single world

. . . .

The way, when we climb a mountain,
Vermont throws itself together. (1989, 140)

The "Vermont" that throws itself together in a moment is already *there* as a *potential*—a *some*thing waiting to happen in disparate and incommensurate objects, registers, circulations, and publics. It's in fall colors, maple syrup, tourist brochures, calendars, snow, country stores. It's in Vermont liberalism but also in the fight over gay marriage. It's in racial homogeneity but also in white lesbian couples with babies of color everywhere you look. It's in the influx of New York wealth long ago rushing in to shore up that certain look of rolling hills and red barns but it's also in the legacy of the dairy industry written onto the landscape and property laws, and in the quirkiness, quaintness, dullness, and violence of village life in this time and place. What interests me about this "Vermont" is not the effort to pin down exactly where it came from—its social construction—but the moment itself when an assemblage of discontinuous yet mapped elements throws itself together into something. Again. One time among many. An event erupting out of a series of connections expressing the abstract idea "Vermont" through a fast sensory relay. Disparate things come together differently in each instance and yet the repetition itself leaves a residue like a track or a habit. Each instance of "Vermont" coming together is a singularity of a cliché but that doesn't mean it's dead or just one example of the same. It remains an event—a moment when something happens to produce the quality of being in a scene. In other words, it's a composition—a poesis—and one that literally can't be seen as a simple repository of systemic effects imposed on an innocent world but has to be traced through the generative modalities of impulses, daydreams, ways of relating, distractions, strategies, failures, encounters, and worldings of all kinds.

There are countless such moments in which something throws itself together—moments that require a kind of weak theory, or a space in which attending to such things is made habitual (Stewart 1996). Not an innocent or uniform space, but one that *takes place* in the course of historical forces such as the collective saturation of the senses, the voracious productivity of the marketing industry, the hard-edged, caste-like quality of relations of race and class, the seamless sprawl of the built environment, the chronotypical changes in time and space, and all the things that happen to the status of the event itself. To inhabit a space of attending to things is to incite attention to co-existing forms of composition, habituation, performance, and event and to the "weak" ontologies of lived collective fictions comprised of diacritical relations, differences, affinities, affects, and trajectories (Stewart 2007). For me, then, the point of theory now is not to judge the value of analytic objects or to somehow get their representation "right" but to wonder where they might go and what potential modes of knowing, relating, and attending to things are already somehow present in them as a potential or resonance.

Take, for instance, the scene in a cafe in a small West Texas town. A biker couple comes in limping. All eyes rotate to watch them as they move to a table and sit down. They tell me they hit a deer coming into town and dumped their bike. The room comes to a dead stop. Slowly, people begin to offer questions from their tables, drawing out the details. Then there are stories about other collisions and strange events at that place on the west road. Some people make eye contact across the room. A *we* of sorts opens, charging the social with lines of potential. I imagine that people will keep their eyes open for bike parts when they travel the west road and that there will be talk about the overpopulation of deer, or the new law legalizing riding motorcycles without a helmet, or speculation about what parts would break in a speeding encounter with a deer caught in a headlight. Or that talk might turn to the image of hitting the open road, or to abstracted principles like freedom, fate, and recklessness. But one way or another, the little accident will compel a response. Shift people's life trajectories in some small way by literally changing their course for a minute. It might unearth old resentments, or set off a search for lessons learned. It might pull the senses into alignment with simple choices like good luck and bad, or polemics about laws and liberties, wild rides, and common sense.

The poesis of the ordinary draws attention and becomes habitual because things don't just *add up*. *Some*thing throws itself together and then floats past or *sticks* for some reason. Some such things have *meaning* per se; most have force in some other form.

Weirdly collective sensibilities seem to pulse in plain sight. A stranger shows up at my door in the middle of the afternoon. She and her husband are thinking of buying the big house across the street. She wants to know if anyone uses chemicals on their lawns, or dryer sheets. At first I have to wonder what a dryer sheet *is*. But then images pop into my head: the sweet smell of dryer sheets coming in with the breeze on a cloudless day, the little orange flags sticking up out of the grass at the schoolyard, warning that chemicals have been sprayed, the ChemLawn trucks parked up on Widows' Hill in front of the places with the big lawns. I mutter some kind of shorthand version of these things to the woman standing at my door, but really all it takes is a *look* and the woman is *gone*, leaving little seeds of anxiety to sprout.

Two middle-aged people sit awkwardly together in a breakfast diner on a town square in Ohio. The thin, blonde, carefully-tanned woman is having a grapefruit. The heavy-set, pasty man is eating biscuits and gravy. It's an odd scene. Clearly their first meeting. The woman is talking about her workout schedule and what she eats. She says she's not obsessive about it but she likes to keep her body in shape. She pulls out bottles of vitamins and herbal supplements. "I take two of these when I wake up, these are with meals, these in the afternoon. These are good for energy if I feel a little low. . . ." She takes out lotions and rubs them into her skin.

He maintains a careful look of interest. But things don't seem to be going well for him.

A few minutes later, the grapefruit woman says to the biscuit man, "Of course, you'd have to lose thirty pounds." He's nodding. "Of course, oh yes." He's looking down at his biscuits and gravy. His eyes wander around the table at a level well below the range of possible eye contact. Then he lowers his head over his plate and eats.

Who knows how these two people found each other. This was before Internet dating (if you can imagine). Maybe they used personal ads in the local newspaper. Maybe they were the only two single, middle-aged people in the county and someone set them up. Whatever it was, it was an experiment. Just to see what would happen. And things were *happening*, all right, even though "*it*" was so "*not* happening*."

Things jump into form, whether the scene is of the beaten-up coal mining camps in West Virginia, or the proliferation of little worlds budding up almost indiscriminately in Las Vegas, or the twisted aspirations of homeless men to inhabit some kind of world, or the way that a spectral apparition of a "mainstream" pops between dream and matter.

Alphonso Lingis noted the jumpiness of social poesis when he was touring a mine at the Arctic Circle:

> the young miner who showed me the mine put out every cigarette he smoked on his hand, which was covered with scar tissue. Then I saw the other young miners all had the backs of their hands covered with scar tissue. . . . when my eye fell on them it flinched, seeing the burning cigarette being crushed and sensing the pain. . . . The eye does not read the meaning in a sign; it *jumps* from the mark to the pain and the burning cigarette, and then jumps to the fraternity signaled by the burning cigarettes. (1993, 296)

The jumpiness of things throwing themselves together has become an object of ordinary attention. That's why models of thinking that glide over the surface of modes of attention and attachment in search of the determinants of big systems located somewhere else are more and more like road blocks to proprioception than tunnels that yield understanding.

The moment when things throw themselves together into something that feels like *some*thing is the kind of cultural production that's often given form in literature and poetry and folklore. Take, for instance, Louise Erdrich's description in *The Painted Drum* of the moment when teenage trouble is collectively sensed on Revival Road in rural New Hampshire:

On my walks I've seen the turbulence of each neighbor child hit like a small quake. . . . Most of the houses on this road are surrounded by a depth of dark trees and a tangle of undergrowth. No two are within shouting distance. Yet you know, merely waving to the parents whose haunted eyes bore through the windshields of their car. You hear, as new trail bikes and motorbikes rip the quiet, as boom boxes blare from their perches on newly-muscled shoulders. The family cars, once so predictable in their routes, buck and raise dust racing up and down the hills. It is a painful time and one averts one's eyes from the houses containing it. The very foundations seem less secure. Love falters and blows. Steam rises from the ditches and sensible neighbors ask no questions. (2005, 13)

What she's describing is a collective sensibility lived in the mode of potentiality—a singular mode of production people *wait* to sense snapping into place. And one that can be signaled in short hand through sensory signs that act as metonymic entry points—almost a metonymic explosion into something that's thrown itself together. This is a kind of knowing akin to Barthes's "third meaning." A significance that's immanent and erratic and evident not in semantics but in the way that something picks up density and texture as it moves through bodies, dramas, and scenes (1985).

In *Atonement,* Ian McEwan describes the migraine of a woman of means in 1935. The migraine is a "black-furred creature beginning to stir":

Habitual fretting about her children, her husband, her sister, the help, had rubbed her senses raw; migraine, mother love, and over the years, many hours of lying still on her bed, had distilled from this sensitivity a sixth sense, a tentacular awareness that reached out from the dimness and moved through the house, unseen and all-knowing. Only the truth came back to her, for what she knew, she knew. The indistinct murmur of voices heard through a carpeted floor surpassed in clarity a typed-up transcript; a conversation that penetrated a wall, or better, two walls, came stripped of all but its essential twists and nuances. What to others would have been a muffling was to her alert senses, which were fine-tuned like the cat's whiskers of an old wireless, an almost unbearable amplification. She lay in the dark and knew everything. (2003, 63)

There's talk here of essences, ontologies, but weak ones. Not just situated or qualified ontologies, but ontologies immersed in the middle of things. An oscillation, a knowing that is *itself* a resonating chamber for what's happening. A contact zone in which what emerges is not a *mirror* of oppression or promise but a *residue* of all the moments of watching and waiting in the mode of the potential, or the very *problem* of a moment of poesis.

A moment of poesis can be a pleasure or a dragging undertow, a sensibility that snaps into place or a profound disorientation. It can endure or it can jump into something new. It can sag, defeated, or harden into little mythic kernels. It can be carefully maintained as a prized possession or left to rot. It can morph into a cold, dark edge, or give way to something unexpectedly hopeful.

It's something that happens. An immersive fiction of being *in* something that feels like *some*thing whether that's a little world with some kind of coherence, or a project of some kind, or a structure of feeling you're stuck in, or a luscious novel, or sobering memoir read two pages a night before falling asleep. It's the effort to stay in a bad relationship, or the upstairs neighbor in Michigan vomiting every morning before going to work in the Ford factory, or the elderly African-American neighbor in West Virginia who kept his windows blacked and sat at night at the far end of the house with his back up against a windowless wall in case there was a racist attack like the one he had suffered forty years earlier. It's my son skipping classes every day to play basketball on the tennis court with his buds and disappearing at night if anyone from the budding neighborhood "gang" calls him to come out and no amount of talk or grounding can pull him back into the *some*thing of our household instead. It's why my five-year-old daughter has to wear pink dresses and pink cowgirl boots and any effort to get pants on her elicits the scream—"I CAN'T BE THE PRINCE!!!" And why, when asked why she doesn't speak Spanish in the school playground, she said, without having to think, "because we don't care."

"Who?"

"Marisol, Ixchel, Dominque y *me*—Ariana. Miss Dulce says 'Las Princessas cowgirls.'

Little fingers. That's what Ixchel does" (she hooks her two little fingers together). "Comprendes?"

"Got it."

A moment of poesis is a mode of production in an unfinished world. A weak theory that builds connections like the one Edward P. Jones both uses and describes in this scene from *The Known World*:

When he, Moses, finally freed himself of the ancient and brittle harness that connected him to the oldest mule his master owned, all that was left of the sun was a five-inch-long memory of red orange laid out in still waves across the horizon between two mountains on the left and one on the right. He had been in the fields for all of fifteen hours; he paused before leaving the fields as the evening rapped itself about him. The mule quivered, wanting home and rest. Moses closed his eyes and bent down and took a pinch of the soil and ate it with no more thought than if it were a spot of cornbread. He worked the dirt around in his mouth and swallowed, leaning his head back and opening his eyes in time to see the strip of sun fade to dark blue and then nothing. . . . This was July and July dirt tasted even more like sweetened metal than the dirt of June or May. Something in the growing crops unleashed a metallic life that only began to dissipate in mid-August, and by harvest time that life would be gone altogether, replaced by a sour moldiness he associated with the coming of fall and winter, the end of a relationship he had begun with the first taste of dirt back in March, before the first hard spring rain (2003, 1–2).

Tracing the worlds that people make out of such contact zones requires a supple attention and the capacity to imagine trajectories and follow tendencies into scenes of their excesses or end points. Mick Taussig, for instance, is driven to an ethnographic fictocriticism to describe the problem of a desperate poesis in Colombia in *My Cocaine Museum*. It's the moment when the agribusiness boom just stopped:

Now there is no work at all. . . . That's all over now. The idea of work work. Only a desperate mother or a small child would still believe there was something to be gained by selling fried fish or iced soya drinks by the roadside, accumulating the pennies. But for the young men *now*, there's more to *life*, and who really believes he'll make it past twenty-five years of age?. . . . At fourteen these kids get their first gun. Motorbikes. Automatic weapons. Nikes. Maybe some grenades as well. That's the dream. Except that for some reason it's harder and harder to get ahold of, and drug dreams stagnate in the swamps in the lowest part of the city like Aguablanca, where all drains drain and the reeds grow tall through the bellies of stinking rats and toads. *Aguablanca*. White water. The gangs multiply and the door is shoved in by the tough guys with their crowbar to steal the TV as well as the sneakers off the feet of the sleeping child; the *bazuco* makes you feel so good, your skin ripples, and you feel like floating while the police who otherwise never show and the local death squads hunt down and kill addicts, transvestites, gays—the *desechables*, or "throwaways"—whose bodies are found twisted front to back as when thrown off the back of pickups in the sugar cane fields owned by but twenty-two families, fields that roll like the ocean from one side of the valley to the other as the tide sucks you in with authentic Indian flute music and the moonlit howls of cocaine-sniffing dogs welcome you. (2004, 19)

I, too, can trace a series of such moments of poesis in West Virginia over the years as things have come together and taken root or fallen apart and modes of cultural production have accrued layers of substance. I was living in the beaten-up fragments of coal mining camps when Reagan was elected and right away the stories started about people getting kicked off social security disability checks. Why her? She's a widow with diabetes, no car, no running water, and no other income. Why him? He's crazy and one-legged, he's got nobody. *Everyone* knew that something was happening, that we were *in* something. Old people were buying cans of dog food for their suppers. The force of things piled up in floods of stories and objects piled up on the landscape like phantom limbs. This was not so much a resistance, or even the resilience of a way of life, but the actual residue of what people there called *making something of things*. My job there was the chronicling of this incessant composition that had sunk into the ground of the place, grown dense and textured until it had come to feel like a trap people were caught in and never wanted to leave.

The choices were stark. Like being a Christian or being a sinner and the two edges touched, the extreme trajectories of potentiality meeting in a circuit. The churches were bad ass—full of wildness, sexual fantasy, bold-faced moves of force, the dripping sweetness of bodies draped on each other in fellowship, and raucous music with unearthly harmonies. Snake handling boomed whenever the economy went bust. For the sinners, there was drinking and drugs and sucking the gas out of other people's cars with a tube. For everyone, eccentricity flowered over time, producing some spectacular old people who had a way with words as thick as magma and all you could do when you were with them was to listen as hard as you could and try to come up with *some*thing to hold up your end of things. The narrative structure of daily stories was almost entirely digressive, haptic. People walked right in on one another without knocking and sat down at the kitchen table without saying a word. Then something would throw itself together. People were living in cars and the stories were tracing their daily progress over the hills—where they were parked, how the babies' dirty diapers were piling up in the back seat. Sometimes there were phantasmagorical eruptions of craziness, maybe a teenager going on a week-long burning spree and ending up living under a rock, or racist violence in the dark, in the woods, in a space of condensed displacement—a white on black rape, all men, an escape, and a long night's walk back to the safety of a segregated camp. Never an official confirmation of any kind.

People were getting killed in the deadly little punch mines. And then it was over. The mines closed when oil prices dropped. Then it was the end of the last big contract strike for the UMW. A group of striking miners sat waiting to see the doctor in the poor people's health clinic, their bodies huddled together. It had just become clear that the strike would fail—fail spectacularly—and everyone was saying that the union was dead and the miners had been reduced to "company sucks." You could feel the stunned defeat settle on the room in a heavy pause filled with the shallow, suffocating breath of black lungs. Then, out of nowhere, Bobby Cadle spun a kind of fairy tale that someday someone was going to scale the high brick walls of Governor Rockefeller's mansion and loot it for all it was worth. The others listened and at the end they were calmer, sitting together as if something had happened. They'd been given a story of power grown palpable as if it could be breached like a wall and then broken up and dispersed like loot. But more than that, it was a little composition to make something *of* the mess they were in, a little *some*thing offered politely, slightly solemnly, like a gift. They were quiet sitting together. I think they probably felt a little more stuck too—that smothering feeling everyone talked about. An attachment to a life in which potentiality and all its trajectories lie buried and resonating in cultural residues piled so high the present reels.

Things throw themselves together but it's not because of the sameness of elements, or the presence of a convincing totality. It's because a composition encompasses not only what has been actualized but also the possibilities of plenitude and the threat of depletion. Matter in an unfinished world is itself indefinite—a *not yet* that fringes every determinate context or normativity with a margin of something deferred or something that failed to arrive, or has been lost, or is waiting in the wings, nascent, perhaps pressing. Benjamin (2003) notes this poesis in the transmogrification of images touching matter.

The allegorical transfixing of history and nature is only one example—one that became explicit in West Virginia in the remembering of named *places* and ruins in the hills where accidents, horrors, encounters, and lost utopias happened. But other things also threw themselves together into affective matter as the place got hit with one thing and then another. When the talk shows started, young people who were overweight or didn't talk right were flown to Hollywood to be *on* them. Fast food chains in town became the only place to work; the beat-up pickups went and the beat-up Ford Escorts came. The idea hit that the young people were all going to have to leave so the girls all started taking Karate lessons in preparation; now there are a lot of black belts in West Virginia. Wal-Mart happened. Oxycontin happened. Tourism *didn't* happen. Falwell's Moral Majority didn't happen either; the little metal stands full of Moral Majority pamphlets appeared in the back of churches but they went untouched and then faded away. The punch mines came back and all the deaths were splayed out for the nation. Mountain top removal came. The kind of utopian thinking that comes of hard drinking flickered on and off through it all like the blue lights of a TV set left on at night.

Vegas, of course, is a different story with different trajectories to trace. And so is the story of the master-planned, and the story of the homeless, and countless other stories that can be told. But they all have their forms of alertness to the poesis of a something snapping into place, if only for a minute. All of these stories of tracing things that come together have their attachments to potentiality and their constant production of the sense of being *in* something—something grand, something degraded, something dumb—whatever. Everywhere now you hear the question "how'd you get into *that*?" Things don't just add up.

References

Barthes, Roland. 1985. "The Third Meaning: Research Notes on Some Eisenstein Stills." In *The Responsibility of Forms: Critical Essays on Music, Art, and Representation*, trans. Richard Howard, 41–47. Berkeley: University of California Press.

Benjamin, Walter. 2003. *The Origin of German Tragic Drama*. Translated by John Osbourne. New York: Verso.

Erdrich, Louise. 2005. *The Painted Drum*. New York: Harper Collins.

Jones, Edward P. 2003. *The Known World*. New York: Harper Collins.

Lingis, Alphonso. 1993. "The Society of Dismembered Body Parts." In *Deleuze and the Theatre of Philosophy*, edited by Constantin Boundas and Dorothea Olkowski, 289–303. New York: Routledge.

McEwan, Ian. 2003. *Atonement.* New York: Anchor Books.

Sedgwick, Eve Kosofsky. 1997. "Paranoid Reading and Reparative Reading: Or, You're so Paranoid, You Probably Think this Introduction Is about You." In *Novel Gazing: Queer Readings in Fiction*, edited by Eve Sedgwick, 1–40. Durham, N.C.: Duke University Press.

Stevens, Wallace. 1989. "July Mountain." In *Opus Posthumous: Poems, Plays, Prose.* New York: Alfred A. Knopf.

Stewart, Kathleen. 1996. *A Space on the Side of the Road: Cultural Poetics in an "Other" America.* Princeton, N.J.: Princeton University Press.

———. 2007. *Ordinary Affects.* Durham, N.C.: Duke University Press.

Taussig, Michael. 2004. *My Cocaine Museum.* Chicago: University of Chicago Press.

KATHLEEN STEWART is Professor of Anthropology at the University of Texas at Austin. She is the author of *A Space on the Side of the Road: Cultural Poetics in an "Other" America* and *Ordinary Affects.* Her current book projects are *Worlding* and (with Lauren Berlant) *The Hundreds.*

11 "Or in Other Words": Recasting Grand Theory

AFTER HAVING READ C. Wright Mills's *The Sociological Imagination* (1959) as a graduate student, for me the term *grand theory* does not evoke awestruck respect so much as an amused memory of Mills poking fun at the grand theorist Talcott Parsons's grandiose prose. In this collection of superb and thought-provoking essays debating the place of grand theory in folklore, Haring and Fine also specifically mention Mills. Close to fifty years have passed since *The Sociological Imagination* was first published. Despite the intervening decades and Mills's dated use of the male pronoun when describing scholars and students alike, many of the eloquent insights contained in that book remain relevant to this discussion. Rereading Mills, I here consider theory not just as a mode of thinking, but also of communicating abstract and general concepts through writing.

Before proceeding further, I should point out that when Alan Dundes (2005) charged that folklorists were endangering the discipline by not generating enough grand theory, he did not use the term in quite the same way as Mills. Dundes praised grand theory in terms of its broad applicability and capacity to deliver otherwise hidden insights. As he wrote, "true grand theories allow us to understand data that would otherwise remain enigmatic, if not indecipherable" (2005, 389). While Mills would no doubt agree on theory's usefulness in bringing hidden issues to light, he less enthusiastically characterized grand theory as primarily "the associating and dissociating of concepts" (1959, 26) and as "a level of thinking so general that its practitioners cannot logically get down to observation" (33). Grand theorists, he charged, never "get down from the higher generalities to problems in their historical and structural contexts" (33). Further,

Mills questioned the intelligibility of grand theory and its tendency to be phrased in the "turgid and polysyllabic prose that seems to prevail in the social sciences" (217). Characterizing Talcott Parsons's theoretical overview expounded in *The Social System* (1951) as a prime example of grand theory, Mills offered mischievous "translations" of Parsons's convoluted pronouncements in clearer language. Mills's critique, then, covers both conceptual substance and rhetorical style. Reflecting on theory—grand or otherwise—I build on Mills's insights to argue for the value of flexibly moving between (1) levels of generality and (2) registers of language.

Pursuing Generality

Taking on the perspective of any interpretive framework is incipiently to engage with a theory, whether this is accepted as part of common-sense knowledge or as the elaborated and specialized domain of initiated academics. As Raymond Williams pointed out in his wonderfully useful *Keywords: A Vocabulary of Culture and Society,* "theory" derives from the Greek *theoros,* "spectator," and by the seventeenth century was set in opposition to practice (1983, 316). Theory, then, suggests the act of stepping back to survey from afar—and frequently from above—so that particulars can be viewed amid larger patterns. Theoretical lenses bring sharper focus to categories and processes that might otherwise blur into the fabric of taken-for-granted realities. Just as spectators look on from particular angles, so too theories represent perspectives embedded in social worlds and power relations, and as such are forms of situated knowledge (cf. Haraway 1988).

The people we meet in the course of fieldwork certainly already carry their own theories. As Margaret Mills pointed out in her survey of feminist theories in folklore, "our data . . . are always already speaking 'theory'—somebody's theory, theory in the everyday—and it's our job to sort out whose theory" (1993, 174). I learned in Alan Dundes's radiantly inspiring classes to always elicit "oral literary criticism," that is, to invite commentary from people who shared folklore forms (cf. Dundes 1966). Remaining attentive to such locally generated theory—and perhaps exploring its more general applications—is a first step towards extending interpretive authority and revisioning "informants" as intellectual collaborators and mentors (Narayan 1995).

The theory encountered through fieldwork, then, might be termed theory from the ground up.

In addition, scholarly training involves acquiring theory from the institution down. To become a member of a discipline, after all, is to learn to wield particular theoretical concepts. Consider, for example, the usefulness of Carl von Sydow's "oicotype," instantly recognizable and illuminating to a trained folklorist, but a funny-sounding word to the uninitiated. The shared concepts of theory allow conversations across diverse examples and locales, creating intellectual community (cf. Fine, this volume). Even as a dominant paradigm like "the philology of the vernacular" guides our training—as Bauman suggests in his brilliant essay in this volume—theoretical conversations generated within other disciplines also may speak to this paradigm. Theory, then, is shared, reworked, and refined within and across disciplinary communities in classrooms, conference rooms, and publications.

Theory grows grander, it seems, as its scope widens across disciplinary boundaries. Quentin Skinner's collection, *The Return of Grand Theory to the Human Sciences* (1985), for example includes theorists—Gadamer, Derrida, Foucault, Lévi-Strauss, and others—who in proposing terms and frameworks that traversed disciplines, achieved extensive intellectual scope and influence. That these exemplars were all male is a different but related question linked to "the gender of theory" (cf. Lutz 1996); while I cannot explore this issue in depth here, it is useful to keep in mind when examining the gender balance in any bibliography, including the ones in this volume.

In C. Wright Mills's formulation, a fascination with data represents a descent from the vertiginous heights of grand theory, and so folklorists engaging with actual practices, texts, and human creativity would, by definition, be sliding away from inclusion in a pantheon of the grand theorists. Whether we pursue "low" theory (in Margaret Mills's terms), or "humble" theory (in Noyes's formulation), or aspire to higher flights of generalization, in adopting theory at all, our challenge is to move beyond what C. Wright Mills termed "the fetishism of the Concept" (1959, 50). While theoretical concepts can illumine, holding on to particular concepts too emphatically can blind. While contemplating empirical materials, it is useful to remain attentive to multiple levels of theory. As Mills eloquently puts it, "The capacity to shuttle between levels of abstraction with ease and with clarity is a signal mode of the imaginative and systematic thinker" (34).

Levels of Language

In his discussion, Mills presented concrete examples of grand theory in the form of selections from Talcott Parsons's classic *The Social System*. Mills reproduced jargon-laden and clause-ridden passages from *The Social System* and then impishly proceeded to provide his own rendition with the phrase, "*Or in other words.*" To offer a complete example of the comic effect of such juxtaposition would take up too much space, but as an illustration, here are the first sentences of a passage from Parsons and its translation by Mills:

> *Parsons writes:*
> Attachment to common values means, motivationally considered, that the actors have common 'sentiments' in support of the value patterns, which may be defined as meaning that conformity with the relevant expectations is treated as a 'good thing' relatively independently of any specific instrumental 'advantage' to be gained from such conformity, e.g., in the avoidance of negative sanctions. . . .

Three long paragraphs in this vein and a lengthy footnote later, Mills offered a pithy paragraph-length translation:

> *Or in other words*: When people share the same values, they tend to behave in accordance with the way they expect one another to behave. . . .
> (1959, 31)

At various junctures, Mills reduced Parsons's 555-page magnum opus into the simple wording of three phrases (31) and four paragraphs (32–33). With these translations, Mills reminded us that while theoretical insights are all too often associated with a ponderous rhetorical style and abstruse language, they can also be expressed in simpler terms.

To enter the world of rationalized theory is usually to adopt what Clifford Geertz (1983), borrowing from the psychoanalyst Heinz Kohut, described as "experience-distant" concepts, as opposed to the "experience-near" concepts moored in the everyday world. We recognize theorists, it seems, partly through the key terms they have invented or have taken out of everyday use to brand with specialized meaning. Geertz's elegant rendering of the distinction between theoretical and everyday language is worth recalling:

> An experience-near concept is, roughly, one that someone—a patient, a subject, in our case an informant—might himself see, feel, think,

imagine, and so on, and which he would readily understand when similarly applied by others. An experience-distant concept is one that specialists of one sort or another—an analyst, an experimenter, an ethnographer, even a priest or an ideologist—employ to forward their scientific, philosophical, or practical aims. "Love" is an experience-near concept, "object cathexis" is an experience-distant one. (1983, 57)

To speak only in experience-near language in scholarly settings can be seen as stubbornly naïve and uninformed; to insist on using experience distant theoretical language to non-scholars can seem bizarrely affected. Zora Neale Hurston's account of her early attempt to study African-American folklore after graduating from Barnard College is a salutatory reminder of the need, in our fieldwork, to switch registers of language, even when scholarly training has made a term familiar enough to be easily spoken:

> I went about asking, in carefully accented Barnardese, "Pardon me, but do you know any folk tales or folk songs?" The men and women who had whole treasuries of material just seeping through their pores, looked at me and shook their heads. No, they had never heard of anything like that around there. Maybe it was over in the next county. Why didn't I try over there? I did and got the self-same answer. Oh, I got a few little items. But compared with what I did later, not enough to make a flea a waltzing jacket. (Hurston 1995 [1942], 687)

As dual inhabitants of everyday and scholarly worlds, we are attuned to the need to shift—or we could say *code switch*—in our choice of words to be effective. Unfortunately, scholars sometimes brandish theoretical terms as a defensive tic, a means of showing off, or even of bludgeoning others into silence, regardless of context. It seems to me that we are best served by consciously and strategically deciding when such terms are useful. When do they offer insights, allowing for generalization across cases, and when do they obscure vivid particulars behind big words? When do the terms of theory enable conversations with work developed in other settings, a shorthand for other scholars, and when do such words self-importantly connote insider-knowledge, scaring off the uninitiated? Margaret Mills's essay in this volume wonderfully reminds us of the multiple ways that the people whom we theorize about might respond to our attempts, from agreement to somewhat puzzled acceptance to correction to complete bafflement. Yet to explain the theoretical ideas at all is already to embark on translation: *Or in other words.*

I teach an ethnographic writing class in which we read portions of Mills's essay "Grand Theory." I then ask students to choose a paragraph from any of the most bewildering, dense theoretical passages they have ever read and to translate, using clearer, more accessible language. This is a useful exercise for wrestling with what these concepts shaped by others really mean. Equally, this practice is useful for one's own writing. For intellectual inclusivity, giving theory the chance to join different conversations, I believe that at least somewhere in a piece of writing we should lay out in simple language just what we mean by a theoretical term, ideally offering a practical example.

Conclusion

The appendix to *The Sociological Imagination* holds another section very worth reading and germane to this discussion: advice to a beginning student titled "On Intellectual Craftsmanship." Here Mills observes that, "the most admirable thinkers within the scholarly community . . . do not split their work from their lives" (1959, 195). He advises that "you must learn to use your life experience in your intellectual work: continually to examine and interpret it. In this sense craftsmanship is the center of yourself" (1959, 196) and he suggests keeping an on-going file of ideas to foster self-reflection and connections.

This creative movement between life experience and intellectual work can also take place, I believe, when traversing levels of theory and choosing registers of conceptual language. Whenever, as scholars, we are faced with communicating our ideas, two guiding questions might be: when are theoretical terms representing particular perspectives useful for the greatest intellectual clarity? When do these terms need clarification for particular audiences we hope to reach? In the spirit of C. Wright Mills, I end with the reminder of the usefulness of sometimes stepping away to rephrase, through a concrete example, or just simpler language: *Or in other words....*

References

Dundes, Alan. 1966. "Metafolklore and Oral Literary Criticism." *Monist* 60: 505–16.
———. 2005. "Folkloristics in the Twenty-First Century (AFS Invited Presidential Plenary Address, 2004)." *Journal of American Folklore* 118 (470): 385–408.
Geertz, Clifford. 1983. *Local Knowledge: Further Essays in Interpretive Anthropology.* New York: Basic Books.

Haraway, Donna. 1988. "Situated Knowledges: The Science Question in Feminism and the Privilege of Partial Perspective." *Feminist Studies* 14: 575–99.

Hurston, Zora Neale. 1995. (1942) "Dust Tracks on the Road." In *Folklore, Memoirs, and Other Writings*, 557–808. New York: The Library of America.

Lutz, Catherine. 1996. "The Gender of Theory." In *Women Writing Culture*, ed. Ruth Behar and Deborah Gordon, 249–66. Berkeley: University of California Press.

Mills, C. Wright. 1959. *The Sociological Imagination*. New York: Oxford University Press.

Mills, Margaret. 1993. "Feminist Theory and the Study of Folklore: A Twenty-Year Trajectory toward Theory." *Western Folklore* 52: 173–93.

Narayan, Kirin. 1995. "The Practice of Oral Literary Criticism: Women's Songs in Kangra, India." *Journal of American Folklore* 108: 243–64.

Parsons, Talcott. 1951. *The Social System*. Glencoe, Ill.: The Free Press.

Skinner, Quentin, ed. 1985. *The Return of Grand Theory to the Human Sciences*. Cambridge: Cambridge University Press.

Williams, Raymond. 1983. *Keywords: A Vocabulary of Culture and Society*. Rev. ed. New York: Oxford University Press.

Kɪʀɪɴ Nᴀʀᴀʏᴀɴ is Professor of Anthropology and South Asian Studies at the Australian National University. She is author of *Storytellers, Saints, and Scoundrels* (winner of the 1990 Victor Turner Prize for Ethnographic Writing and cowinner of the Elsie Clews Parsons Prize for Folklore); *Mondays on the Dark Night of the Moon: Himalayan Foothill Folktales* (with Urmila Devi Sood); *Love, Stars, and All That*; *My Family and Other Saints*; *Alive in the Writing: Crafting Ethnography in the Company of Chekhov*; and the forthcoming *Everyday Creativity: Singing Goddesses of the Himalayan Foothills*.

12 Disciplining Folkloristics

But when one draws a boundary it may be for various kinds of reason. If I surround an area with a fence or a line or otherwise, the purpose may be to prevent someone from getting in or out; but it may also be part of a game and the players be supposed, say, to jump over the boundary.

— Ludwig Wittgenstein, *Philosophical Investigations,*
§499 (1953, 138–39)

I MUST ADMIT that my excitement in contributing to a debate regarding the place of theory in folkloristics is tempered by lingering frustration. Forging more prominent spaces for theoretical work in folkloristics has been one of my central goals for two decades. A decade and a half ago, Amy Shuman and I published a set of papers on theory in *Western Folklore* (Briggs and Shuman 1993). But here's the rub: Shuman and I attempted to turn these articles into a collection for classroom use, but we were repeatedly told by publishers that there is no market for books on folkloristic theory. Seeking to disprove this assessment, in 2003 Richard Bauman and I published a book exploring how the study of folklore has informed canonical epistemologies and political projects of the modern world for three centuries. I wish I could say that *Voices of Modernity* stimulated broad rethinkings of the politics and poetics of the discipline and sparked new attempts to insert folkloristics more centrally in interdisciplinary theoretical debates.

I thus could not have been more pleased to see my predecessor in the directorship of the University of California, Berkeley Folklore Program, Alan Dundes, deliver a spirited call for theoretical debate to a packed ballroom at the 2004 AFS meeting. I applaud organizer Lee Haring, *Journal of Folklore Research* editor Moira Smith, and the other contributors for responding to Dundes's challenge. Starting with Mills's provocative questioning of the category of theory, the authors insightfully query the theory/folklore relationship, examining how the constitution of these categories overdetermines their interrelations. I would like to further explore this reluctance to embrace theory.

I draw on science studies, especially Thomas Gieryn's (1983) notion of "boundary-work." In the mid-twentieth-century United States, Richard Dorson and other folklorists developed a largely a-theoretical form of boundary-work that successfully delimited an autonomous folkloristics and expanded its resource base and academic authority. Subsequently, the ethnography-of-speaking and performance-centered approaches in folklore fostered an opposing rhetorical style that used theoretically-engaged analysis to promote creative exchanges across disciplinary boundaries. Pointing out why these rhetorics seem less viable in the twenty-first century as discipline-building strategies, I suggest an alternative approach that fosters innovation by collaborating on theoretical issues with non-academics who reflect deeply on the poetics and politics of vernacular culture—people we used to call "the folk."

Science-studies critiques have become markers of academic importance, even for disciplines that also situate themselves in the humanities. But my goal is not just to put folkloristics on the science-studies map but to reflect on folklorists' discipline-building practices and their viability within contemporary academic and socio-political contexts—and to imagine alternatives.

Boundary-Work as Disciplinary Strategy

Acknowledging Dorson's role in consolidating U.S. folkloristics, Simon Bronner (1986) sagely shows that his influence emerged less from new theoretical visions than tireless efforts to promote folkloristics, particularly by creating academic controversies. Science studies can bring Dorson's contribution clearly into focus. As Gieryn elucidates in his classic article, boundary-work is a rhetorical style that constructs social boundaries, demarcating intellectual activities accorded the prestige of science from non-science or pseudo-science. Boundary-work is most commonly used "to enlarge the material and symbolic resources of scientists or to defend professional autonomy" (782).

It builds individual reputations and expands disciplinary boundaries by claiming authority and resources from other professions.

In *The British Folklorists*, Dorson tells the story of John Aubrey's discovery of a preexisting object—folklore: "With the sure instinct of the tradition-hunter, he recognized the rupture in society caused by new inventions and new political forms, and the damaging effect of these innovations on the old peasant culture" (1968, 5). Discovering folkloristics' object required a distinct set of methods, collecting "at first hand, from his own immediate world" (1968, 8). The precarious, evanescent nature of folklore required boundary-work—distinguishing the true object from superficially similar forms. As Latour (1987) suggests, a key feature of scientific work is the generation of textual-cum-social networks. Modes of collecting, classifying, and comparing empirical objects and transforming them into texts thus created social/textual networks or communities, first antiquarian and later folkloristic. Dorson traces connections from Aubrey's foundational instincts to their institutionalization in a science of folklore, professional societies, a specialized literature, and increasingly explicit, standardized methods adopted by scholars—a network that seemed to grow continuously through space and time. Boundary-work is hard-wired into Dorson's origin story of folkloristics, seemingly required by the nature of folklore and the folk. In the preface, Dorson describes "the brilliant history of folklore science in England" as a model for folklorists in Europe, Asia, Africa, and the United States (1968, v). The dissemination of folkloristics reproduced boundary-work globally.

When he turned to the United States, Dorson similarly labored to consolidate folkloristics as a discipline and demarcate its boundaries. His attacks on amateurs, popularizers, the mass media, and academic interlopers helped to professionalize the discipline, defining folklorists through the ability to recognize a distinctive object, develop distinctive methods, and form professional networks of folklorists. Second, Dorson argued that "the study of American folklore was being invaded by commercializers and could not as yet be protected by scholars, since specialists in American folklore had not yet been trained" (1971, 7). The production of legitimate knowledge about American folklore thus required departments of folklore and professorial positions; only scholars who gained entrance into this network through professional training could defend folklore's boundaries.

Just as scholarly authority over "folklore" marked the disciplinary boundary from within, Dorson's explicitly polemical concept of "fakelore" drew it from without, demonizing commercialization, the mass media, "frivolous" folklore investigations, and scholars from other disciplines who "dabbled with folklore" (7) as possessors of mere fakelore.

The contributors to this issue present a rich array of reasons that theory has played a limited role in North American folkloristics. The power of boundary-work in mid-twentieth-century folkloristics brings the issue into focus. The fate of folkloristics depended, Dorson claimed, on laying exclusive claim to distinct objects, methods, professional societies, texts, and departments—not theories. The papers in which Dorson claimed theoretical ground, "A Theory for American Folklore" (first published in 1959) and "A Theory for American Folklore Reviewed" (first published in 1969), are exceptions that prove the rule. They were specifically intended to provide "common theoretical ground" for American folklorists (47). In the 1960s, anthropology, linguistics, sociology, literary studies, and other disciplines were redefining themselves in theoretical terms. Dorson explicitly distinguished himself from "a modish cult—say of symbolic structuralism, or sociopsychodynamics, or linguistic folklife, or computerized mythology" (51). Echoing American exceptionalism, Dorson rejected foreign theories in favor of a construction of theory that starts with examples of American folklore, proposes "definitions, the necessary precursor to any theory" (50), and ends up by contributing to "a cooperative inquiry" that will "illuminate the American mind" (48). Even this self-proclaimed turn to theory extended Dorson's boundary-work by adopting a narrowly inductive, not to mention nationalist, understanding of theory that was explicitly defined in opposition to the definitions of theory that were galvanizing and redefining other disciplines. U.S. folklorists could not simply become part of the global expansion of British folkloristics. Building a discipline from made-in-the USA folklore created a boundary vis-à-vis European folkloristics: high theory was to remain on the other side of the Atlantic.[1]

Departing somewhat from the other contributors here, I suggest that the question is not just whether folklorists produce or use theory but its marginality to discipline-building. Placing boundary-work at the core of discipline-building strategies produced a strong sense of commitment and esprit de corps; nevertheless, as Fine points out, theory plays a crucial role in providing intellectual cohesion and coherence. Uniting around objects, methods, and a zealous commitment to protect the discipline against usurpers is less successful in fostering broad participation in intellectual debates.

Here I note a contradiction in Dundes's role in the field, evident in the article that sparked this special issue. Dundes became the major successor to his teacher in continuing Dorson's role as folkloristics' primary boundary-worker.[2] Most folklorists attribute Dundes's inability to promote theory to having bet on the wrong theoretical horse. Nevertheless, the tremendous importance of psychoanalysis in history, literature, feminist studies, and other fields in recent decades would suggest that the case is not so simple. Indeed, bringing new interpretations of Freud, Jacques Lacan (1977 [1966]), and other psychoanalysts into folkloristics could have created theoretical dialogues across disciplines. I would rather argue that Dundes's difficulties in generating more interest in theory emerges from his persistent efforts to press boundary-work as the sine qua non for discipline-building—or, increasingly, discipline-preservation—strategies for folkloristics. By definition, central reliance on boundary-work produces, in Noyes's terms, provincial intellectuals, defined through their (self-)exclusion from what they characterize as metropolitan sites of high theory production.

During the Cold War expansion of scientific ideologies and resources in the mid-twentieth century, the boundary-work passionately undertaken by Dorson and some of his students expanded disciplinary autonomy, scholarly authority, academic departments and programs, grants, and public recognition. The unstable "poetics of disappearance" (Kirshenblatt-Gimblett 1998a) that defined a continuously vanishing object helped create and naturalize new forms of modernity (Bauman and Briggs 2003). In a post-Cold War, postmodern, fragmenting, and rapidly-shifting world, the market for modernities collapsed and then restructured. The juxtaposition of closely-guarded boundaries and claims to scholarly authority with the erosion of resources and prestige sparked a proliferation of declensionist disciplinary narratives—folklorists' dysfunctional tales of woe. Following up on a point by Bauman, communicative technologies were often used as means of demarcating the boundary of folklore—through their placement on the other side. Accordingly, practitioners could not claim shifting and productive relationships to new technologies as scholarly sites—even as Hermann Bausinger (1990) was convincing European folklorists of their productivity.[3]

Drawing on science studies, rhetorical, genealogical, Marxist, feminist, postcolonial, and other critical modes, the disciplines of anthropology, American Studies, and geography gained new ground by transforming foundational concepts from neutral, objective tools *for* inquiry into objects *of* critical inquiry. These approaches have reimagined intellectual disciplines as practices that often overlap with lay, technical, and corporate pursuits and with one another. While some folklorists have followed suit (Bendix 1997; Kirshenblatt-Gimblett 1998b; Shuman 2005; Stewart 1994), the field has largely clung tightly to folklore as an actually existing object that can be located, collected, classified and analyzed. In academic institutions increasingly embracing neoliberalism, folklorists' assertions of entitlement to former positions and resources have lost ground to fields making stronger claims on broader intellectual and social/political landscapes. At the turn of the millennium, inhabiting shifting boundaries and generating new, cross-disciplinary strategies have become more successful than holding onto fixed boundaries and static concepts. A folkloristics created by boundary-work has become unsustainable.

Theoretical Boundary-Crossing as Disciplinary Strategy

The experience of the 1960s and 1970s suggests, however, that folkloristics can generate substantial academic authority creating analytical models that generate dialogic zones with adjacent disciplines—in short, in theoretically-inspired boundary-*crossing*. Dell Hymes (1974) placed folklore and folkloristics at the center of the "ethnography of speaking," infusing a new analytic perspective that galvanized research in anthropology, communication, linguistics, and folkloristics with such central notions as genre, repertoire, community, and transmission.[4] Hymes (1981) and Bauman (1977) then used the notion of performance in redefining and reinterpreting folklorists' objects of study.

Two features are crucial here. First, whether or not one wants to call these frameworks "theory," they generated broad textual networks through shared analytic principles. Second, rather than defending boundaries, folklorists drew on concepts and modes of analysis from anthropology, literary studies, linguistics, and history, and they convinced other scholars that folkloristics was valuable for their own fields of inquiry. The cross-disciplinary dialogue that took place in the 1980s in the *Journal of American Folklore*, the cross-disciplinary popularity of folklore courses, the demand for folklorists in other departments, and the emergence of symposia and special issues on performance in adjacent fields indicate the success of this opposing mode of discipline building. Theoretically-oriented folklorists seemed to have been clearly aware during this period that theory is, as Fine suggests, productive of social-textual networks.

Nonetheless, my goal, to brutalize Shakespeare, is not to praise Bauman and Hymes and bury Dorson. Indeed, more theoretically- or analytically-based strategies have their drawbacks, too, and these are tied to the epistemological and social underpinnings of the very notion of theory. As Mary Poovey (1998) shows, the theory/fact opposition is a quintessentially modern artifact, reflecting an Enlightenment conviction that facts can exist apart from interests, opinions, and epistemological positions and that general propositions occupy a privileged sphere that is not contingent on history or politics. What gets defined as "theory" is what can best dress itself up as rational, general, disinterested, abstract, and universal—that is, as quintessentially modern and "Western." As Mills observes, theory is markedly interdiscursive, explicitly tied to other academic texts; it is also metadiscursive, defining, limiting, and regulating what counts as scholarly discourse within a particular field. What is perhaps most crucial for folkloristics is that the social location of the author helps decide what gets classified as "theoretical": the words of white, male senior professors from leading U.S. or European universities are much more likely to be dubbed theoretical (I write self-reflexively) than those of women of color, scholars in institutions that lack graduate programs, or nonacademics.

Notions of "high," "middle," and "low" presuppose this privileging of seemingly decontextualized, abstract discourse, project spatial/social relations in epistemological terms, and reproduce the scale-making claims of theory—the idea that it can enable us to jump from universalities to particularities and back without losing our balance. I would locate the politics of theory less in *theories* as epistemological objects than in *theorizing*, in discursive practices that both produce certain types of formulations and frame them as theory. Theoretical discourse is thus potentially exclusionary, expelling merely empirical, classificatory, or methodological work and creating hierarchically-ordered textual networks—with the generators of theories on top, their authorized interpreters next, those charged with "applying" them to data just below, and researchers seemingly ignorant of or incapable of citing theory on bottom. Hierarchies of prestige in academic institutions, within nations and between them, get naturalized in the process.

Roberts's essay indicates how closely theorizing reproduces racial inequalities. The continuing force of three centuries of identifying the speech of white, elite, Euro-American males with rationality, abstraction, and the unmarked subject and of identifying the speech of women, the working classes, and people of color with concreteness, "the local," and marked subjects (Bauman and Briggs 2003; Shapin 1994) is painfully captured by the marginalization of work on African-American folklore and the fate of Américo Paredes's *With His Pistol in His Hand* (1958). Half a century ago, Paredes reconceptualized folklore as politically-charged expressive forms that define the shifting borders of conflict, difference, and oppression. Some of Paredes's colleagues and students incorporated these insights (see Bauman 1971; Bauman and Abrahams 1981; Limón 1994), but most folklorists continued to embrace a consensus model built around a reified, depoliticized notion of folklore. If folklorists had followed Paredes's lead, I suspect that the field would be enjoying a much stronger position in the contemporary academic landscape which, as Roberts (1999; this volume) suggests, is centrally concerned with cultural pluralism. Rather, as José Limón notes, Paredes has been expunged from genealogies of folkloristics (2007).

Theory-based modes of disciplining folkloristics can thus be as exclusionary as boundary-work-centered strategies. Although one or the other tends to predominate at particular times and within specific textual-social networks, they intersect and overlap in complex ways, reproducing social and epistemological hierarchies and obstructing creativity. According to boundary-making perspectives, only professional folklorists can discover a ready-made object and then collect, classify, entextualize, analyze, and compare it. From the theory-centered perspective, analytic principles are generated in academic settings and used in determining which phenomena are "theoretically relevant." These strategies converge in generating scholarly narratives that cast non-academics as makers of folklore and academics as producers of folkloristic knowledge.

Missing here are some the key sources of theoretical or analytic creativity in the field. I have worked on the folklore of Spanish-speaking areas of New Mexico and a region in Venezuela where Warao (an indigenous language) is spoken. In both, I could only begin to comprehend the vast amount of knowledge that shaped everyday life after I apprenticed myself to intellectuals, individuals recognized as reflecting actively and creatively on social life and its discursive representation. George and Silvianita López in New Mexico and Santiago and María Rivera in Venezuela had contemplated for decades the aesthetic features and social/political impact of the discursive genres they performed.[5] In researching proverbs, legends, curing songs, laments, and other forms, I spent years with them, participating in daily life, recording and transcribing performances, and collaborating in interpretive work. The Lópezes had attended elementary school, but the only formal education open to the Riveras (brother and sister) were the English classes that I provided. With all four I entered into discussions of quite abstract and complexly interdiscursive formulations that explicitly served metadiscursive functions, seeking to define, interpret, and regulate everyday discourse. Trying to understand Mrs. López's proverb performances, for example, involved a radically different way of defining proverbs and tracing their rhetorical effects (Briggs 1988). I did not *find* discursive objects—they *told* me what I should collect. I am not suggesting that my analyses flowed directly from their perspectives; my interpretations rather emerged by bringing their words into dialogue with philosophy, history, folkloristics, anthropology, ethnic and racial studies, ethnomusicology, and other fields.

Both boundary-work and the folklorist-as-theorist perspectives teach us to approach "informants" as purveyors of folklore who lack the ability to consciously analyze forms—and who are therefore positioned outside folkloristics' boundary. Scholars who follow these ideologies commonly draw on their collaborators' analytic reflections but fail to acknowledge their role in the work of theorizing. In doing so, they reproduce racial, national, class, and professional hierarchies and commit serious lapses of professional ethics by failing to acknowledge intellectual debts. Noyes may indeed be correct in asserting that folklorists suffer from an "inferiority complex" vis-à-vis other scholars, but both Dorson's attacks on "amateurs" and "popularizers" and the general failure to acknowledge "folk" collaborators would suggest (to follow the psychoanalytic logic) a form of compensation that results in a superiority complex in relation to non-academic theoreticians.

Both boundary-work and theory-driven approaches also fall short by failing to grasp how "the object" often contains "the theory." Bauman and I have drawn on Bakhtin (1981, 1986) in suggesting that performances are not snapshots of a particular moment in time but complex cartographies of the movement of discourses, subjectivities, and politics between contexts, genres, and texts (Bauman and Briggs 1990; Briggs and Bauman 1992). Texts themselves are thus both interdiscursive and metadiscursive, attempting to shape how participants will "read" prior discourse and how they will project what is said or written into the future. In many cases, these inter- and metadiscursive cartographies achieve a high level of abstraction and generality. In short, "the theory" can be right there in "the data." Folklorists, as Dell Hymes (1975, 1981) reminds us, are taught to look closely at texts not just as aesthetic or ethnographic objects but also as sources of insight into social life and ways of interpreting it (see also Abrahams 2005).

Beyond Boundary-Work and Theory-Based Hierarchies in Folkloristics: A Proposal

I would like to provocatively lay out some proposals:

1. *Theory is dead! Long live theory!* Insofar as "theory" is defined in Enlightenment terms and is tied to means of generating and naturalizing practices of exclusion and subordination, folklorists should rightly reject "grand theory" and its less pretentious equivalents. Here I stand with Haring in echoing literary theorists who reject the use of theory as a means of regulating scholarly writing axiomatically.

2. Nevertheless, I am not arguing against theorizing. Without powerful inter- and metadiscursive principles we must rely on boundary-work to generate debates that renew disciplinary objects and methods. Nor do I wish to rule out discipline-building practices altogether, strategies for refashioning folkloristics and

efforts to secure resources and authority. I think rather that we should develop new disciplinary practices that depend neither on boundary-work nor standard theory-building modes.

3. One way that folklorists can take the lead in redefining and re-positioning the category of theory is to document *practices of vernacular theorizing*, metadiscourses that are excluded from the communities that are created, as Fine (this volume) suggests, by academic theorizing; here we can follow up on Abrahams's (2005) and Bauman's (this volume) attention to vernacular understandings of cultural forms. We must tread carefully here, because reified understandings of theory's opposite, whether defined as "local," "lived world," or "vernacular," are just as much products of modernity as are "theory"; embracing them uncritically thus involves presupposing and privileging theoretical concepts. Vernacular is defined in opposition to something else; vernacular *versus* cosmopolitan distinctions reproduce local *versus* global, concrete *versus* abstract dichotomies that have sustained the opposition between modernity and traditionality for three centuries (Bauman and Briggs 2003). In order to keep from reproducing social and epistemological hierarchies, we will need to extract the term *vernacular* from its opposition to *cosmopolitan* and the entailed denial of generality, abstractness, and explanatory capacity to vernacularity and its conferral on cosmopolitanism (Briggs 2005).

4. The question remains as to the relationship between *vernacular theorizing* and *theorizing the vernacular*, which is what we are doing in this volume. Rather than viewing their differences and similarities in relativist or comparative terms, I suggest tracing the intersections and exchanges that take place between them. If we examine folkloristics, performance, and vernacular theorizing as practices for producing, circulating, and receiving knowledge, we can examine how they differentiate themselves as well as how they intersect and interact. Once we bring other disciplinary (academic) and institutionally-based knowledge-making practices (as developed by public folklorists and others) into the debate, we will have powerful new ways of articulating what folklore and folkloristics can offer other disciplines and institutions— which is crucial for the future of the profession. Fostering

juxtapositions between knowledge-making practices across the lines of discipline, class, race, nation, and professional status will generate novel approaches.

If "theory" is identified by its social location and its ability to present itself as abstract, rational, and general, then Noyes is probably right that folklorists will find it difficult to compete with psychology or sociology. Nevertheless, if, as Haring argues, the Chartists and 1960s folklorists strove to democratize the notion of creativity, perhaps it is our major calling now to democratize the notion of theory, to acknowledge the crucial theoretical insights that we gain from vernacular intellectuals. Mills interestingly asks who gets credit for generating interdisciplinary ideas; I would like to extend this question to interlocutors classified as non-academics.

I have not offered "a new theory" of folkloristics here. My goals are more modest, at the same time that they are not simply "methodological." I hope to have identified the major impediment to theory-building in the discipline—too great a reliance on boundary-work—and suggested why this practice is partially responsible for disciplinary setbacks, especially in the United States. I pointed to the centrality of folklorists' participation in interdisciplinary theory-building in giving rise to junctures during the twentieth-century in which folkloristics enjoyed academic visibility and institutional strength. Suggesting that conventional understandings of "theory" and who gets recognized for doing it can also be exclusionary and hierarchicalizing, I urged the creation of a broader community of theorists. Such a community would include practitioners in other disciplines and thinkers heretofore barred from academic networks. I argue that links should be created through detailed attention to how different theoretical communities produce knowledge, how discourses and practices move between them, and the differences of power and political economy that shape who gets credit for theorizing and gets to claim their formulations as intellectual property.

Here we can fruitfully bring Wittgenstein into our network. Knocking down all boundaries—folding folkloristics into anthropology, cultural studies, performance studies, or cross-disciplinary programs—would undermine its intellectual locus as a unique crossroads between vernacular theorists and theorists of the vernacular. We need new theories, and making and debating them will require new spaces for theorizing, for creatively rethinking the concepts, practices, rhetorics, and objects of folkloristics and imagining how they can inform and be informed by the profound transformations of culture and capital, bodies and labor taking place in the contemporary world. This project will require institutional recognition and support, from foundations state, agencies, and non-governmental and international organizations, as well as from universities, which, in turn, will require boundaries: there needs to be a there *there* for researchers to be taken seriously. Rather than creating boundaries based on discrete, fixed objects and methods and spending our time defending them, trying to keep folklorists in and intruders out, we might take a clue from Wittgenstein's epigraph and focus on maintaining a flexible, playful relationship to boundaries, jumping over them in such a way as to link and enrich the games being played on both sides.

Acknowledgments

I would like to thank Richard Bauman, Regina Bendix, and Lee Haring for helpful comments on a previous draft. Elizabeth Kelley brought the Wittgenstein quote to my attention.

Notes

1. Here Dorson replays Henry Rowe Schoolcraft's textual nationalism (Bauman and Briggs 2003, ch. 7).

2. See Dow's anecdote in which Dundes repeatedly asks German scholars "'Where's the folklore?'" Dundes's boundary-work often took the form of a statement: "That's not folklore!" He begins his essay with a declensionist story in which the erosion of clear disciplinary boundaries has resulted in a "sad situation" in which "there is no longer a purely separate, independent doctoral program in folklore per se anywhere in the United States" (2005, 385).

3. Dundes (1980, 17) provides an important exception here.

4. Hymes's ability to cross disciplinary boundaries and reconfigure work within them is signaled by his election to the presidencies of the American Folklore Society, the American Anthropological Association, and the Linguistic Society of America.

5. Doctors, epidemiologists, lawyers, and politicians have also been my collaborators in theorizing cultural forms over the years.

References

Abrahams, Roger D. 2005. *Everyday Life: A Poetics of Vernacular Practices.* Philadelphia: University of Pennsylvania Press.

Bakhtin, M. M. 1981. *The Dialogic Imagination: Four Essays.* Translated by Caryl Emerson and Michael Holquist, ed. Michael Holquist. Austin: University of Texas Press.

———. 1986. "The Problem of Speech Genres." In *Speech Genres and Other Late Essays.* Edited by Caryl Emerson and Michael Holquist, 60–102. Austin: University of Texas Press.

Bauman, Richard. 1971. "Differential Identity and the Social Base of Folklore." *Journal of American Folklore* 84: 31–41.

———. 1977. *Verbal Art as Performance.* Prospect Heights, Ill.: Waveland.

Bauman, Richard, and Roger D. Abrahams, eds. 1981. *"And Other Neighborly Names": Social Process and Cultural Image in Texas Folklore.* Austin: University of Texas Press.

Bauman, Richard, and Charles L. Briggs. 1990. "Poetics and Performance as Critical Perspectives on Language and Social Life." *Annual Review of Anthropology* 19: 59–88.

Bauman, Richard, and Charles L. Briggs. 2003. *Voices of Modernity: Language Ideologies and Social Inequality.* Cambridge: Cambridge University Press.

Bausinger, Hermann. 1990. *Folk Culture in a World of Technology.* Translated by Elke Dettmer. Bloomington: Indiana University Press.

Bendix, Regina. 1997. *In Search of Authenticity: The Formation of Folklore Studies.* Madison: University of Wisconsin Press.

Briggs, Charles L. 1988. *Competence in Performance: The Creativity of Tradition in Mexicano Verbal Art.* Philadelphia: University of Pennsylvania Press.

———. 2005. "Genealogies of Race and Culture and the Failure of Vernacular Cosmopolitanisms: Rereading Franz Boas and W. E. B. Du Bois." *Public Culture* 17 (1): 75–100.

Briggs, Charles L., and Richard Bauman. 1992. "Genre, Intertextuality, and Social Power." *Journal of Linguistic Anthropology* 2: 131–72.

Briggs, Charles L., and Amy Shuman, ed. 1993 *Theorizing Folklore.* (Special issue) *Western Folklore* 52 (2–3): 3, 4.

Bronner, Simon. 1986. *American Folklore Studies: An Intellectual History.* Lawrence: University Press of Kansas.

Dorson, Richard. 1968. *The British Folklorists: A History.* Chicago: University of Chicago Press.

———. 1971. *American Folklore and the Historian.* Chicago: University of Chicago Press.

———. 1959. "A Theory for American Folklore." *Journal of American Folklore* 72 (285): 197–215.

———. 1969. "A Theory for American Folklore Reviewed." *Journal of American Folklore* 82 (325): 226–44.

Dundes, Alan. 1980. *Interpreting Folklore.* Bloomington: Indiana University Press.

———. 2005. "Folkloristics in the Twenty-First Century (AFS Invited Presidential Plenary Address, 2004)." *Journal of American Folklore* 118 (470): 385–408.

Gieryn, Thomas F. 1983. "Boundary-Work and the Demarcation of Science from Non-Science: Strains and Interests in Professional Ideologies of Scientists." *American Sociological Review* 48: 781–95.

Hymes, Dell. 1974. *Foundations in Sociolinguistics: An Ethnographic Perspective.* Philadelphia: University of Pennsylvania Press.

———. 1975. "Folklore's Nature and the Sun's Myth." *Journal of American Folk-lore* 88 (350): 346–69.

———. 1981. *"In Vain I Tried to Tell You": Essays in Native American Ethnopoetics.* Philadelphia: University of Pennsylvania Press.

Kirshenblatt-Gimblett, Barbara. 1998a. "Folklore's Crisis." *Journal of American Folklore* 111 (441): 281–327.

———. 1998b. *Destination Culture: Tourism, Museums, and Heritage.* Berkeley: University of California Press.

Lacan, Jacques. 1977. [1966] *Écrit: A Selection.* Translated by Alan Sheridan. New York: W. W. Norton.

Latour, Bruno. 1987. *Science in Action: How to Follow Scientists and Engineers through Society.* Cambridge, Mass.: Harvard University Press.

Limón, José E. 1994. *Dancing with the Devil: Society and Cultural Poetics in Mexican-American South Texas.* Madison: University of Wisconsin Press.

———. 2007. "Américo Paredes: Ballad Scholar." *Journal of American Folklore* 120 (475): 3–18.

Paredes, Américo. 1958. *With His Pistol in His Hand: A Border Ballad and Its Hero.* Austin: University of Texas Press.

Poovey, Mary. 1998. *A History of the Modern Fact: Problems of Knowledge in the Sciences of Wealth and Society.* Chicago: University of Chicago Press.

Roberts, John W. 1999. ". . . 'Hidden Right Out in the Open': The Field of Folklore and the Problem of Invisibility." *Journal of American Folklore* 112 (444): 119–39.

Shapin, Steven. 1994. *A Social History of Truth: Civility and Science in Seventeenth-Century England.* Chicago: University of Chicago Press.

Shuman, Amy. 2005. *Other People's Stories: Entitlement Claims and the Critique of Empathy.* Urbana, Ill.: University of Illinois Press.

Stewart, Susan. 1994. *Crimes of Writing: Problems in the Containment of Representation.* Durham, N.C.: Duke University Press.

Wittgenstein, Ludwig. 1953. *Philosophical Investigations.* Translated by G. E. M. Anscombe. Oxford: Basil Blackwell.

CHARLES L. BRIGGS is the Alan Dundes Distinguished Professor of Folklore in the Department of Anthropology of the University of California, Berkeley. His books include *Competence in Performance* (winner of the Chicago Folklore Prize), *Stories in the Time of Cholera* (with Clara Mantini-Briggs, winner of the J. I. Staley Prize), *Voices of Modernity* (with Richard Bauman, winner of the Edward Sapir Award), and in 2016, *Tell Me Why My Children Died* (with Clara Mantini-Briggs) and *Making Health Public* (with Daniel C. Hallin). He is currently completing a book that rethinks psychoanalytic folkloristics, folklore and colonialism, and folkloristic approaches to health.

Afterwords

Reflections on Grand Theory, Graduate School, and Intellectual Ballast

IN THE FALL of 2010, I began graduate school in the Department of Folklore and Ethnomusicology at Indiana University. The distance between that point and this seems unreal. As a first generation college student for whom graduate education was once only a vague possibility, it is shocking to glance backward at the ground I have covered. Where my existential questions used to concern how I fit into academia, they now concern how I connect to the life I lived before becoming a folklorist.

When I defended my dissertation in the summer of 2015, many friends asked me how I felt. I told them it was as though I had summited a mountain. Some would then ask what was next. I could not forecast the immediate future, but I knew for certain that there were no more mountains to climb. Nothing will be more formative than finishing that doctorate. Instead, I look forward with a sense of growth. I think about how I might cultivate a fulfilling life with the tools I have been given.

Some of the oldest of these tools come from the pages of the *Journal of Folklore Research*, Volume 45, Number 1. Known in graduate student vernacular as "the grand theory issue," or simply "grand theory," this is a seminal collection for my cohort of folklorists and ethnomusicologists. A big reason for this, as Michael Dylan Foster and Ray Cashman note in their preface, is ubiquity. At Indiana, articles from this issue are regularly included on graduate seminar syllabi. I think I was assigned to read "The Philology of the Vernacular" at least three times in as many years of coursework. But the reason for this issue's ubiquity is good. In addition to making provocative arguments of their own, the authors of the essays in the grand theory issue cut through the differences that might seem to set folklorists apart from one another. They address us as a community rather than a confederacy of experts in oral tradition, material culture, ritual and festival, and the like.

Such a sense of solidarity is important for beginning graduate students. Many of us felt adrift as we started our doctoral or master's studies at Indiana, but the grand theory issue gave us something to hold onto as we developed our intellectual identities. Whatever else was true of our varied interests, we could unite over the ideas presented here. The essays are broad enough to encompass any facet of verbal, material, or customary folklore studies, yet they are refined enough to appeal directly to folklorists. And together, they present a template for how to do our kind of work. What are we talking about when we talk about grand theory? It is a metaphor that can be used to explain folklore on a phenomenological basis (Mills 2008). What is the danger of grand theory? It can exert an undue, even terrible influence in the wrong cultural or political circumstances (Dow 2008). How can folklorists communicate across disciplines? We must absorb and make use of the theoretical structures of our fellow experts in expressive culture (Narayan 2008). The list goes on, but I will not continue it here.

I will say, though, that these sorts of reflections provided intellectual ballast at a time when I felt in constant danger of going overboard. They helped me find a center when other readings were either too deeply situated in a longstanding dialogue or, frankly, written without beginners in mind. Dorothy Noyes's "Humble Theory" was a particularly important touchstone in this regard. When I felt overwhelmed, I could lean heavily on those 2,300 words to remind myself that, no matter how intense the challenge, I was learning the business of going out into the world, figuring out how people understood their place in it, thinking about their perspectives, and interpreting them. The muscular brevity and merciful clarity of the essay were reminders that the *raison d'etre* of my disciplinary community is to get as close as possible to the cultures we choose to study. This was the attitude that I then adopted and brought with me to the seminar room in those early days of doctoral school. Whether we were reading Dorson or Durkheim, my professors and colleagues could expect me to "Humble Theory" our subject matter for the week.

I recall that I was directed to read "Humble Theory" in two separate seminars during my first semester. In the second, we had the privilege of speaking to Dorothy Noyes during a live phone call to Ohio State University. Imagine my disappointment when she gently disavowed her excellent work. I remember her words exactly: "Actual scholarship is harder than cheerleading in ten pages." I was a little crushed, but in retrospect, I can see what she was trying to say. The piece is less an analytical case study than a rallying cry for folklorists. Like much of the material in this collection, it is meant to get us thinking about our place in the academy and the field. And, bless her, Dorry was nudging us first-year students to look beyond her invigorating remarks—to take what she had to say into our work with us but not to rest on it as an end unto itself. This seems to be a marker of many of the essays collected here. They are prescient, punchy overviews of some aspect of our discipline, and they act as nourishment to the ailing researcher. I recall that Ray Cashman once described "The Philology of the Vernacular" as an "espresso shot" of ideas that he goes to when his folkloristic sensibilities get groggy. I know what he means.

That the grand theory issue is being repackaged as a standalone volume is a testament to its importance. With this project, it takes its place among other formative volumes, like *Eight Words for the Study of Expressive Culture* (Feintuch 2003), and for an earlier generation of folklorists, *Toward New Perspectives in Folklore* (Paredes and Bauman [1972] 2000), both of which grew from issues of the *Journal of American Folklore*.[1] Through the grand theory issue, the *Journal of Folklore Research* has provided a system of scholarly paths for folklorists and ethnomusicologists who have come of age since 2008, and for those coming of age now. It is good and fitting that it should be published as a book in the Indiana University Press series *Encounters: Explorations in Folklore and Ethnomusicology*. Future researchers will surely find purchase in its words.

My encounters with the grand theory issue continue even now. In February of 2016, I accepted a position as Program Director for Folk and Traditional Arts at the Maryland State Arts Council. Tasked with grants administration, festival planning, and the management of regional partnerships in the documentation and promotion of folklife, I crisscross the state on a weekly basis. On a Monday, I might be hashing out the best way to divvy up tent space among screen painters, piñata makers, and competitive marble players. On a Friday, I might be hunched over a Marantz, trying not to breathe as my consultant weeps at the thought that someone appreciates his music enough to want to be his apprentice.

I do not want to suggest that the words of the grand theory issue echo in my head in these moments, or during the many other duties I perform every week. This simply is not the case. However, if I do a smidge of autoethnography, I can say that the *ideas* of the grand theory issue are with me constantly. They inhere in the way I perceive the field of folklore studies at large: in the way I do fieldwork, in my methods for identifying folklore, and in my choice whether or not to intellectualize an issue in public or private discussion. In practice, I am a folklorist because I went to graduate school for folklore studies. In theory, however, I am a folklorist because I have internalized the scholarly traditions set out in the pages of this volume. I seldom think of particular passages anymore because the perspectives offered here have become so fundamental to the way I engage with my work. This is certainly the mark of an important treatise. Not to discount the efforts of others, but how many publications function as common parlance in our scholarly community? As a recent PhD in folklore studies, I am so pleased to see this issue being recognized for its remarkable contribution.

Note

1. These were the *Journal of American Folklore* (108) 430 and (84) 331, respectively.

References

Bauman, Richard. 2008. "The Philology of the Vernacular." *Journal of Folklore Research* 45 (1): 29–36.

Dow, James R. 2008. "There is No Grand Theory in Germany, and for Good Reason." *Journal of Folklore Research* 45 (1): 55–62.

Feintuch, Burt, ed. 2003. *Eight Words for the Study of Expressive Culture.* Urbana: University of Illinois Press.

Haring, Lee. 2008. "America's Antitheoretical Folkloristics." *Journal of Folklore Research* 45 (1): 1–9.

Mills, Margaret A. 2008. "What('s) Theory?" *Journal of Folklore Research* 45 (1): 19–28.

Narayan, Kirin. 2008. "'Or in Other Words': Recasting Grand Theory." *Journal of Folklore Research* 45 (1): 83–90.

Noyes, Dorothy. 2008. "Humble Theory." *Journal of Folklore Research* 45 (1): 37–43.

Paredes, Américo, and Richard Bauman, ed. (1972) 2000. *Toward New Perspectives in Folklore.* Bloomington, Ind.: Trickster Press.

CHAD EDWARD BUTERBAUGH is Program Director for Folk and Traditional Arts and Co-Director of Maryland Traditions at the Maryland State Arts Council.

Ten Years After

A DECADE AFTER the conference panel that engendered these papers, what a pleasant surprise to find the late Benedict Anderson agreeing with me: "Americans are not naturally given to grand theory. A glance across the social sciences and humanities for the 'great theorists' of the past century makes this abundantly clear." Then he lists six philosophers, five historians, five sociologists, and five anthropologists, ending his list with Bakhtin, de Man, and Barthes, and writes, "All the foundational figures are European" (2016, 15). In the previous generation, folklorists did not move towards an autonomous methodology (Paredes and Bauman 1972), or even towards theorizing. No one tried out Jacques Derrida's deconstruction of Claude Lévi-Strauss's structuralist treatment of myth; no one tackled Robert Plant Armstrong's reverent treatment of the effect of material culture on receivers, contemporary though it was with the reader-response theories being developed for literature (Derrida 1978; Armstrong 1971). After the conference, a wise colleague whispered to me that the grand theory for folkloristics was already present, if not acknowledged.

When Dell Hymes advocated "the study of communicative behavior with an esthetic, expressive, or stylistic dimension" (1975, 350), he had long envisaged a larger field that would embrace folkloristics. That took shape under the limited name "ethnography of speaking" (Hymes 1974), but if it was to encompass transcription, translation, and publication, it would have to admit writing and revive Hymes's earlier term, "ethnography of communication" (1964). Years later he could still call for it "to go beyond case studies to comparison and the greater precision and depth of analysis which comparison and contrast of types of case makes possible . . . ; to use the generalized framework in our own society, as part of the development of social theory; to apply a critical, reflexive perspective to its own work" (Hymes 1996,

103). But Hymes's attempt to create a unified, autonomous field, in which folklore, linguistics, and cognitive studies would feel at home, failed (Duranti 1997, 13). Instead, the ethnography of speaking inspired the widest variety of investigations (Bauman and Sherzer 1989), and it was the Parry-Lord-Foley oral composition theory that moved toward autonomy through accumulating case studies (Foley 1988, 94–111).

Given the indisposition of Americans to theorizing, what is left is "that middle territory between grand theory and local interpretation" (Noyes 2008, 41; see also chapter 6). Several emerging fields offer to fertilize that territory. One is creolization studies, which have hardly begun to theorize, but which are already saying that the renegotiation of culture, including folklore, is a heightened way of seeing ordinary cultural process, taking account of power differentials and their effect on cultural production (Baron and Cara 2011). A second way of theorizing folklore is seeing it through the lens of translation studies. Why not view transmission, the movement of a piece of expressive culture from one performer to another, as a kind of translation? In both fields, scholars examine the ways in which people (1) acting for themselves (2) move cultural products they perceive or classify as (3) traditional, or worthy of transmission, between (4) different systems of communication. Both fields know that their work "changes everything" (Venuti 2013). Finally, the verbal-art allotment in that middle territory can welcome the discoveries of cognitive linguistics, especially cognitive poetics (Stockwell 2002). Its notion of conceptual metaphor can be applied to finding the underlayer behind the metaphors in verbal art that voice cultural preferences (Kövecses 2007). That middle territory will bear rich theoretical fruit when scholars traverse the boundaries between these fields. Their dialogues could stimulate another conference.

References

Anderson, Benedict. 2016. "Frameworks of Comparison." *London Review of Books* 38 (2): 15–18.

Armstrong, Robert Plant. 1971. *The Affecting Presence: An Essay in Humanistic Anthropology.* Urbana: University of Illinois Press.

Baron, Robert, and Ana C. Cara, eds. 2011. *Creolization as Cultural Creativity.* Jackson: University Press of Mississippi.

Bauman, Richard, and Joel Sherzer. 1989. "Introduction to the Second Edition." In *Explorations in the Ethnography of Speaking*, edited by Richard Bauman and Joel Sherzer, ix–xxvii. Cambridge: Cambridge University Press.

Derrida, Jacques. 1978. "Structure, Sign and Play in the Discourse of the Human Sciences." In *Writing and Difference*, trans and additional notes Alan Bass, 278–93. Chicago: University of Chicago Press.

Duranti, Alessandro. 1997. *Linguistic Anthropology.* New York: Cambridge University Press.

Foley, John Miles. 1988. *The Theory of Oral Composition: History and Methodology.* Folkloristics. Bloomington: Indiana University Press.

Hymes, Dell. 1996. *Ethnography, Linguistics, Narrative Inequality: Toward an Understanding of Voice.* London: Taylor and Francis.

———. 1975. "Folklore's Nature and the Sun's Myth." *Journal of American Folklore* 88 (350): 346–69.

———. 1974. "Ways of Speaking." In *Explorations in the Ethnography of Speaking*, edited by Richard Bauman and Joel Sherzer, 433–51. Cambridge: Cambridge University Press.

———. 1964. "Introduction: Toward Ethnographies of Communication." Special issue, "The Ethnography of Communication," *American Anthropologist* 66 (6): 1–34.

Kövecses, Zoltán. 2007. *Metaphor in Culture: Universality and Variation.* Cambridge: Cambridge University Press.

Noyes, Dorothy. 2008. "Humble Theory." *Journal of Folklore Research* 45 (1): 37–43.

Paredes, Américo, and Richard Bauman, eds. 1972. *Toward New Perspectives in Folklore.* Austin: University of Texas Press.

Stockwell, Peter. 2002. *Cognitive Poetics: An Introduction.* London: Routledge.

Venuti, Lawrence. 2013. *Translation Changes Everything: Theory and Practice.* London: Routledge.

LEE HARING is Professor Emeritus of English at Brooklyn College of the City University of New York. He has carried out folklore research in Kenya, Madagascar, Mauritius, and the other islands of the Southwest Indian Ocean. He is the author of *Stars and Keys* (IUP, 2007), a collection of folktale translations from the Indian Ocean islands; *Verbal Arts in Madagascar;* the online book *How to Read a Folktale* (http://www.openbookpublishers.com/product/109/), which translates a heroic epic from Madagascar; and numerous scholarly articles.

Index